THE STORIES BEHIND THE NUMBERS

DATA-DRIVEN DECISIONS:
Making Better Decisions Using Insights

ROY OKONKWO

Copyright © 2023 All rights reserved.

Roy Okonkwo.

Data-Driven Decisions: Making Better Decisions Using Insights

No part of this publication may be reproduced, distributed, or transmitted in any form or by any means, including photocopying, recording, or other electronic or mechanical methods, without the prior written permission of the publisher, except in the case of brief quotations embodied in critical reviews and certain other noncommercial uses permitted by copyright law.

ISBN: 978-5-5714-3011-1

Globally available

Cover design by Emphaloz Publishing House

Disclaimer: The content of this book is provided for informational and educational purposes only. The author and publisher make no representations or warranties regarding the completeness, accuracy, or applicability of any strategies or techniques contained within. Readers should use their own judgment and consult with professionals before applying the methods discussed. The author and publisher disclaim any liability for any direct, indirect, or consequential damages resulting from the use of this material.

FOREWORD

In a world awash with information, the ability to distill data into meaningful insights is more crucial than ever. Welcome to **The Stories Behind the Numbers**, where I invite you to embark on a journey that transforms the way you approach decision-making. As a data scientist, I've seen firsthand how the power of data can illuminate paths we never knew existed. This book is not just about statistics and algorithms; it's about weaving narratives that help us make sense of the chaos around us. Every number tells a story, and understanding these stories empowers you to make informed choices in your everyday life.

REVIEWS

Chidera N., Lagos, Nigeria

"A Master class in Data-Driven Decision Making!"

I was initially intimidated by the thought of diving into a book about data, especially since I have limited experience in the field. However, "The Stories Behind the Numbers" broke everything down in a way that was approachable and fascinating. What really stood out for me was the author's ability to show how data is not just for businesses or tech companies but also for individuals in their everyday lives. As someone interested in becoming more data-literate, this book provided me with practical examples that I could immediately apply, whether in analyzing personal finance, making better career decisions, or even predicting market trends.

The blend of theory and relatable application, along with the ethical discussions on the power of data, is incredibly important for anyone looking to understand the current landscape. I would highly recommend this to anyone interested in data analytics or who simply wants to make more informed decisions in their personal and professional life.

Amaka O., Abuja, Nigeria

"An Eye-Opening Journey into the World of Data!"

This book is a breath of fresh air. As a business consultant in Nigeria, I often encounter data, but "The Stories Behind the Numbers" showed me how much more powerful data-driven decisions can be. The author does an excellent job of bridging the gap between complex data science concepts and everyday examples. Each chapter not only explained core concepts like predictive analytics and artificial intelligence but also painted a clear picture of how these tools can be used in everyday situations.

I was particularly impressed with the author's focus on the ethical implications of data usage. In Nigeria, data privacy and accountability are major concerns, and reading this book made me reflect on how organizations, especially in emerging markets, need to approach these issues more thoughtfully. This book is an essential read for anyone looking to make smarter, more ethical decisions using data.

Michael T., London, UK

"Practical, Insightful, and Highly Relevant!"

I've been working in data analytics for years, but "The Stories Behind the Numbers" still managed to teach me a few things I didn't know. The author strikes the perfect balance between being technical and accessible. Whether you're a beginner or have experience in the field, this book has something valuable for you. I especially appreciated the practical examples as the book doesn't just discuss theoretical models but shows how they are applied in situations.

One of the key highlights for me was the section on integrating AI and predictive analytics into decision-making. It helped me see how emerging technologies are transforming sectors like healthcare, finance, and marketing in a more impactful way than I had realized. The author's writing is both clear and engaging, which made complex topics easy to digest. Highly recommend for anyone looking to improve their decision-making through data insights!

Dr. Ifeanyi O., Chief Data Scientist, Lagos, Nigeria

"An Exceptional Guide to Data-Driven Leadership and Decision Making"

In my role as a Chief Data Scientist, I have read many books on data science and analytics, but Roy's book stands out as an exceptional resource. What sets this book apart is the author's ability to demystify complex topics without oversimplifying them. Whether it's predictive analytics, machine learning, or artificial intelligence, the book offers clear, actionable insights on how these technologies can be applied to decision-making across various sectors.

Moreover, the author brings an important perspective to the table by addressing the ethical dimensions of data usage. Too often, we focus on the technical aspects and overlook the impact of our decisions on society and individuals. This book is a timely reminder that ethical considerations must be at the core of data-driven decision-making. For any data professional, this book provides both practical and thought-provoking content that encourages a deeper understanding of data's potential and responsibility.

Dr. Sandra L., Director of Analytics & AI, New York, USA

"A Thoughtful Exploration of Data's Role in shaping tomorrow's Decisions"

As someone deeply involved in AI and efficient decision-making, I was thoroughly impressed by "The Stories Behind the Numbers". The author brings an impressive breadth of knowledge to the subject, addressing everything from the technical intricacies of machine learning to the societal implications of data analytics.

What really resonated with me, however, was the focus on human-centric decision-making. Too often, discussions around data are entirely focused on the tools and models themselves, but this book reminds us that the ethics of data especially in terms of privacy, transparency, and bias must never be an afterthought. The chapter on AI ethics is especially noteworthy, offering a strong framework for data scientists to consider how their work impacts individuals and communities. This is a must-read not only for those looking to understand the power of data but for those who want to apply it in a responsible and ethical way.

This combination of practical guidance and ethical reflection ensures that the book appeals to a wide audience, from data enthusiasts looking to understand the basics to professionals seeking to deepen their expertise and apply it responsibly.

ABOUT THE AUTHOR

Roy Okonkwo is a seasoned data scientist, strategist, and entrepreneur with a passion for transforming raw data into actionable insights that drive meaningful decisions. With years of experience in the fields of data analytics, machine learning, and artificial intelligence, Roy has worked with organizations across various industries, helping them harness the power of data to optimize operations, improve customer experiences, and solve complex problems.

A true advocate for data-driven decision-making, he believes that data has the potential to empower individuals and businesses alike. His deep understanding of both the technical aspects of data science and the ethical implications of its use informs his approach to responsible innovation. Beyond his work with clients, he is a thought leader and educator, dedicated to sharing his knowledge through workshops, speaking engagements, and writing. He is passionate about demystifying data and making it accessible to a broader audience, from novices to industry professionals.

When he's not immersed in data, Roy enjoys exploring the intersection of technology, business, and social impact, with a particular interest in how data can drive sustainable, ethical growth in emerging markets.

Contents

Foreword iii

Reviews iv

About The Author viii

Contents ix

Chapter One: Decoding The Data: Understanding Its Language 1

Chapter Two: From Raw Numbers To Rich Narratives 20

Chapter Three: The Art Of Asking The Right Questions 36

Chapter Four: Patterns And Predictions: Finding Clarity In Chaos ... 42

Chapter Five: Bias And Belief: The Hidden Influences On
Decision Making 60

Chapter Six: Visualizing Insights: Seeing Beyond The Numbers 73

Chapter Seven: Integrating Ethics In Data 88

Chapter Eight: Everyday Analytics: Making Data Work For You ... 109

Chapter Nine: Collaborative Intelligence: Harnessing Collective
Insights 119

Chapter Ten: The Future Of Decision-Making: Embracing Data-Driven
Mindsets 128

CONCLUSION 146

CHAPTER ONE

Decoding The Data: Understanding Its Language

In an era where data is often heralded as the new oil, the ability to understand its language has become more vital than ever. Data literacy, defined as the ability to read, work with, analyze, and argue with data, is essential for navigating our increasingly complex information landscape. It empowers individuals to make informed decisions based on evidence, fostering critical thinking, and reducing the risks associated with misinformation and bias.

Data literacy empowers individuals by enabling them to comprehend and question the information they encounter daily. In a world inundated with data from social media feeds to financial reports, this critical skill helps mitigate the pitfalls of misinformation. Consider the myriad decisions we make that are influenced by data, whether it's choosing a healthcare provider based on patient satisfaction scores or selecting a product based on consumer reviews. Empowerment through knowledge enhances our ability to engage meaningfully with the world around us. As industries and daily life become more data-driven, the relevance of data literacy grows. Sectors such as healthcare, finance, marketing, and education increasingly rely on data to drive their operations and decisions. For instance, in healthcare, providers analyze patient data to improve outcomes and tailor treatments. In marketing, businesses harness consumer data to create targeted campaigns. By examining how data literacy influences consumer choices, policy-making, and strategic initiatives, we can appreciate its significance in our everyday lives.

One of the most compelling arguments for data literacy is its impact on decision-making. Understanding and interpreting data accurately can transform how we make choices, shifting from instinctual or intuition-based decisions to evidence-based strategies. For example, a business that uses data analytics to inform its product development is more likely to meet consumer needs than one that relies solely on gut feelings. By showcasing scenarios where data-driven decisions outperformed intuition-based ones, we can see the tangible benefits of leveraging data effectively.

To develop this skill, we must first understand its key components. This includes grasping different types of data such as structured versus unstructured, categorical versus continuous and recognizing how these distinctions affect analysis. Understanding the nuances of these structures, such as databases and spreadsheets, helps individuals better organize and utilize information.

Basic statistical concepts also form the backbone of data literacy. Familiarity with terms like mean, median, mode, standard deviation, and correlation enables individuals to interpret data meaningfully. By demystifying these concepts with relatable examples and simple calculations, we can make statistics accessible to readers of all backgrounds.

Data visualization skills play a crucial role in conveying insights effectively. Well-designed visualizations can illuminate complex datasets, making them easier to understand at a glance. By exploring common visualization tools and techniques, we can emphasize the importance of clarity and accuracy in representing data. Critical thinking and analytical skills are indispensable in analyzing data. A data-literate individual approaches data with a questioning mindset, seeking patterns, outliers, and potential biases. Cultivating a data-literate mindset involves nurturing curiosity and a willingness to learn. By promoting an inquisitive attitude toward the data encountered in daily life whether in news articles, business reports, or social media individuals can begin their journey toward data literacy. Practical exercises, such as keeping a journal or engaging in discussions about data, can further ignite curiosity.

Moreover, data literacy is not a one-time achievement but an ongoing journey. Resources for continuous learning abound, from online courses to podcasts and books. Sharing personal anecdotes or testimonials from individuals who have successfully improved their data literacy can inspire persons to invest in their growth. Collaboration also enhances this skill. Working alongside others can lead to deeper insights and understanding. Engaging with communities focused on data literacy whether online forums or local meetups can create an environment of shared learning and growth.

This concept is a foundational skill in today's world, one that equips individuals to navigate the complexities of information and make informed decisions. By embracing the challenge of becoming more data-literate, readers can transform their decision-making abilities and contribute to a more informed society. The journey begins with curiosity and a commitment to continuous learning, setting the stage for a more engaged and empowered approach to using information.

To fully comprehend the processes in analysis, understanding the distinction between quantitative and qualitative data is foundational. These two types of data serve different purposes, and recognizing their unique characteristics allows us to choose the right approach for our specific analytical needs. By diving into the definitions, applications, and implications of each type, we can better appreciate how data shapes our insights and decision-making processes.

Quantitative data is numerical and can be measured or counted. It is often represented in the form of numbers and can be used to perform mathematical calculations, making it invaluable in various fields, including science, finance, and marketing. Quantitative data can be further categorized into two main types: discrete and continuous data.

Discrete data refers to countable values that are distinct and separate. For example, the numbers of students in a classroom or the number of cars in a parking lot are discrete data points. This type of data is often represented using whole numbers and cannot be broken down into smaller units without losing its meaning. Continuous data, on the other hand, represents measurements that can take on any value within a given range. Examples include height, weight, temperature, and time. Continuous data can be infinitely divided, allowing for a more nuanced analysis. For instance, a person's height can be measured to the nearest centimeter, millimeter, or even more precisely.

Quantitative data is powerful because it allows for statistical analysis and mathematical modeling. Techniques such as regression analysis, correlation coefficients, and descriptive statistics rely heavily on numerical data to derive meaningful conclusions. This objectivity makes quantitative data particularly appealing for decision-makers who seek to minimize bias and uncertainty.

This type is prevalent across numerous sectors. In healthcare, for example, it is used to track patient outcomes, assess treatment effectiveness, and manage resources. Hospitals may analyze patient admission rates and treatment success rates to optimize care delivery. In finance, quantitative data is essential for analyzing stock market trends, forecasting economic indicators, and managing investment portfolios. Financial analysts rely on numerical data to make informed decisions that impact organizational profitability. In marketing, businesses utilize quantitative data to gauge consumer behavior, measure campaign effectiveness, and optimize pricing strategies. Metrics such as conversion rates, customer acquisition costs, and return on investment (ROI) are all based on quantitative analysis. By employing tools like surveys and analytics software, marketers can quantify customer preferences and trends, allowing for data-driven strategies that resonate with their target audiences.

Qualitative data, in contrast, is descriptive and conceptual. It captures qualities or characteristics that are not easily quantifiable. Qualitative data is often gathered through open-ended questions, interviews, focus groups, and observations, providing rich, contextual insights into human behavior and experiences. This type of data is typically non-numeric and can include text, images, or videos.

It is valuable for understanding the "why" behind behaviors, motivations, and perceptions. Unlike quantitative data, which focuses on numerical relationships, qualitative data emphasizes depth and context. It allows researchers to explore complex issues, revealing nuances that numbers alone cannot convey. In social sciences, qualitative data is essential for exploring human experiences and cultural phenomena. Researchers may conduct interviews or focus groups to understand how individuals perceive a particular issue, such as mental health stigma or community engagement. These insights are vital for developing effective interventions and policies that resonate with the affected populations.

In market research, qualitative data plays a crucial role in uncovering consumer preferences and motivations. Focus groups and in-depth interviews can reveal how consumers feel about a brand, product, or service, providing context that quantitative data may overlook. For example, while a survey may indicate that 70% of consumers prefer a specific product feature, qualitative interviews can reveal the underlying reasons for this preference, such as emotional connections or past experiences.

While quantitative and qualitative data are often viewed as distinct and separate, they are best understood as complementary approaches. Each type of data offers unique strengths that, when combined, provide a more comprehensive understanding of a given issue.

One is data triangulation. This involves using multiple data sources or methods to enhance the credibility and validity of research findings. By integrating quantitative and qualitative data, researchers can validate their findings through cross-verification. Second is enhanced decision-making. Combining both data types can lead to more informed decision-making. For example, a business may use quantitative data to analyze sales trends and identify areas for improvement. Qualitative data can then provide insights into customer preferences, helping the company tailor its products or services to better meet consumer needs. Third is providing a holistic understanding. By employing both quantitative and qualitative methods, researchers can gain a holistic understanding of complex issues. This comprehensive approach allows for a richer exploration of problems, enabling organizations to develop strategies that address the root causes rather than just symptoms. Despite the valuable insights these types of data offer, each type also presents unique challenges that must be considered.

For quantitative data, some common challenges include over-simplification, quality and integrity. One potential pitfall of relying solely on quantitative data is the risk of oversimplifying complex issues. While numbers can reveal trends and patterns, they may not capture the full context or underlying motivations behind those trends. Ensuring the quality and integrity of quantitative data is paramount. Errors in data collection, processing, or analysis can lead to misleading conclusions and flawed decision-making.

In qualitative data, challenges include subjectivity and generalization. Qualitative data is inherently subjective, as it relies on individual perspectives and interpretations. This subjectivity can introduce bias, making it essential for researchers to employ rigorous methodologies and reflective practices. Findings from qualitative research may not always be generalizable to larger populations due to the often-limited sample sizes and contexts involved. Researchers must acknowledge these limitations when drawing conclusions.

To effectively utilize both forms, it is essential to adopt best practices that enhance data literacy and foster a deeper understanding of each type's strengths and limitations. Organizations should cultivate a data-driven culture that values both quantitative and qualitative insights. By encouraging open dialogue about data and its implications, organizations can foster a mindset of inquiry and critical thinking among their teams. Providing training and educational resources on data literacy can empower individuals to effectively engage with both types of data. Workshops, seminars, and online courses can help build skills in data collection, analysis, and interpretation. Organizations should strive to integrate quantitative and qualitative data sources into their decision-making processes. This integration can involve cross-functional teams that bring together diverse perspectives and expertise, ensuring that both data types inform strategic initiatives.

Understanding the differences between quantitative and qualitative data is fundamental to effective data literacy. Each type of data offers unique insights and advantages, and when used in tandem, they can provide a more comprehensive understanding of complex issues. By recognizing the strengths and limitations of each type, individuals and organizations can make informed decisions that are grounded in evidence and context.

Data Collection Methods

This is a fundamental aspect of data-driven decision-making, serving as the foundation for analysis and insight generation. The methods used to collect data can significantly influence the quality and relevance of the findings. In this section, we will explore various data collection methods, categorizing them into qualitative and quantitative approaches. We will discuss their respective advantages and limitations, providing guidelines for effective implementation.

The collection involves the systematic gathering of information from various sources to answer research questions, test hypotheses, or evaluate outcomes. The choice of method often depends on several factors, including the research objectives, the nature of the data needed, the available resources, and the specific context of the inquiry. Effective data collection is not merely about gathering data; it requires careful planning, execution, and ongoing evaluation to ensure that the data collected serves its intended purpose.

Quantitative data collection methods focus on gathering numerical data that can be statistically analyzed. These methods are often used in studies that seek to measure variables, identify patterns, and test relationships. One of the most common quantitative methods is surveys and questionnaires. These tools typically consist of a structured set of questions designed to gather specific information from respondents. Surveys can be administered in various formats, including online, paper-based, or face-to-face.

Surveys offer several advantages. They are scalable, allowing researchers to reach many respondents, which makes it easier to gather data from diverse populations. The structured nature of surveys also promotes standardization, enabling uniform data collection that simplifies comparison of responses. Furthermore, responses can be easily quantified and analyzed using statistical methods. However, surveys also have limitations. They may not capture the complexities of respondents' opinions or experiences if the questions are too rigid. Additionally, response bias may occur, as respondents might provide socially desirable answers or misinterpret questions, leading to inaccurate data.

Another quantitative method is experimentation, which involves manipulating one or more variables to observe the effects on other variables. This method is commonly used in scientific research to establish causal relationships. The advantages of experimental methods include a high level of control over confounding variables and the ability to demonstrate cause-and-effect relationships, providing strong evidence for conclusions. However, ethical considerations may arise in some experiments, particularly in fields like psychology or medicine. Moreover, results from controlled environments may not always translate to real-world settings, limiting general application.

Observational methods represent another quantitative approach, wherein researchers systematically watch and record behavior or events as they occur in natural settings. This method is particularly useful in studies where direct measurement is challenging. Observations provide realism, capturing behavior in real-world contexts and revealing insights that surveys or experiments might miss. However, observer bias can influence data collection and interpretation, and the limited scope of observations may not provide data on the motivations or thoughts behind behaviors. Finally, secondary data analysis involves using existing datasets collected for purposes other than the current research question. This method can be cost-effective, as it saves time and resources compared to primary data collection. Secondary data often includes large samples, increasing the potential for generalized insights. However, the existing data may not perfectly align with the current research question, and the quality and reliability of secondary data can vary, affecting the validity of findings.

Qualitative data collection methods focus on gathering non-numerical data to explore complex phenomena, uncover motivations, and understand experiences. These methods provide depth and context, enriching the overall analysis. One common method is interviews, which involve direct, one-on-one interactions between the researcher and the participant. Interviews can be structured, semi-structured, or unstructured, depending on the level of flexibility desired.

Interviews offer depth of insight, allowing for in-depth exploration of participants' thoughts and feelings. The flexibility of this method enables the interviewer to adapt questions based on participants' responses, uncovering unexpected insights. However, conducting and analyzing interviews can be time-consuming, and the interviewer's presence and behavior can influence participants' responses, potentially introducing bias. Focus groups are another qualitative method that brings together a small group of participants to discuss a specific topic. A facilitator guides the conversation, encouraging interaction and dialogue among participants. Focus groups capitalize on group dynamics, stimulating discussion and generating diverse perspectives. This method also allows for efficient data collection from multiple participants simultaneously. Nevertheless, some participants may dominate the conversation, silencing others' perspectives, and groupthink may limit the diversity of responses.

Case studies involve an in-depth exploration of a specific individual, group, or situation. This method is often used in social sciences and can incorporate multiple data collection techniques. Case studies provide a holistic understanding of the subject, including context, processes, and outcomes. However, findings from case studies may not be applicable to broader populations, and the researcher's interpretations can influence the analysis.

Ethnography represents another qualitative approach that involves immersive observation of a particular culture or social group. Researchers spend extended periods in the field, gathering insights through participant observation and informal interviews. Ethnography captures the complexities of social interactions and cultural practices, providing a rich narrative of participants' lived experiences. However, this method is time-intensive and may pose challenges related to the researcher's presence and interpretation.

Selecting the appropriate data collection method is crucial for obtaining valid and reliable insights. Several factors should be considered in this process. First, clearly defining the research objectives and the type of data needed is essential. For example, if the goal is to quantify customer satisfaction, a survey may be the best choice. Conversely, if the aim is to explore motivations behind consumer behavior, interviews or focus groups might be more appropriate.

The nature of the data is another important consideration. Researchers must determine whether quantitative or qualitative data is more suitable for addressing the research question. Some questions may require a mixed-methods approach, combining both types of data to gain a comprehensive understanding. Resources and constraints also play a critical role in the decision-making process. Evaluating the available resources, including time, budget, and personnel, can help identify the most feasible methods. Additionally, ethical considerations must be assessed, as research involving vulnerable populations may necessitate additional safeguards to ensure participants' rights and well-being. Finally, practicality should inform the choice of method. Some methods may be logistically challenging or unsuitable for certain populations, making it important to consider the specific context of the research.

Regardless of the data collection method employed, ensuring data quality and integrity is essential. Several key strategies can enhance the reliability and validity of collected data. Conducting pilot tests of surveys, interviews, or focus groups can identify potential issues and refine the data collection process. This step is crucial for clarifying questions and improving overall data quality.

Training data collectors is another important strategy. Comprehensive training ensures that individuals involved in data collection understand the methodology, ethical considerations, and how to minimize bias. Implementing quality control measures can monitor data collection processes, with regular reviews of collected data for accuracy and consistency.

Documentation of the process is vital for maintaining transparency. Researchers should document protocols, challenges encountered, and adjustments made throughout the study. This transparency enhances the credibility of the findings. After data collection, performing data cleaning to address inaccuracies, missing values, or outliers is essential. Validation techniques, such as cross-referencing with other data sources, can further enhance data integrity.

Data collection methods are critical to the success of data-driven decision-making. By understanding the strengths and limitations of various quantitative and qualitative methods, organizations can select the most appropriate techniques for their research objectives. Effective data collection ensures the reliability and relevance of findings, ultimately leading to informed decisions that drive success.

Institutions leverage data to gain insights, optimize processes, and drive innovation. However, despite its transformative potential, the landscape of data-driven decision making is often clouded by misconceptions that can hinder effective utilization. Understanding and overcoming these misconceptions is crucial for individuals and organizations aiming to harness the power of this information effectively.

- **Misconception 1:** Data Equals Truth: One of the most pervasive misconceptions in the realm of data is the belief that data itself is infallible, that it represents an objective truth. This notion can lead to a dangerous over-reliance on data without considering the broader context in which it was collected. Data is a reflection of reality, but it is not reality itself. Misinterpretations can arise from various factors, including data quality, collection methods, and the inherent biases of those analyzing the data. For instance, data can be skewed by sample selection bias, where the data collected does not accurately represent the population being studied. This can occur if certain groups are overrepresented or underrepresented, leading to flawed conclusions. Furthermore, even well-collected data can be misinterpreted. For example, correlation does not imply causation; just because two variables are correlated does not mean that one causes the other. Failing to recognize this distinction can lead to misguided strategies and decisions.

   To overcome this misconception, it is essential to approach data critically. Organizations should implement rigorous quality checks and ensure that the collection methods are robust and transparent. Contextualizing data is equally important; analysts should consider the circumstances under which the data was gathered, including potential biases and limitations. Engaging diverse perspectives in data interpretation can also help mitigate the risks of misinterpretation. By fostering a culture of inquiry and critical thinking, organizations can ensure that they do not fall prey to the trap of assuming that data is synonymous with truth.

- **Misconception 2:** More Data is Always Better: Another common misconception is the belief that having more data automatically leads to better decision making. While it is true that access to extensive datasets can enhance insights, an overwhelming volume of data can also lead to analysis paralysis, where decision-makers become overwhelmed by the sheer amount of information available. In such cases, the quality and relevance of the data take precedence over quantity. Organizations may find themselves inundated with data from various sources, creating confusion rather than clarity. For example, a retail company might collect data from customer transactions, website interactions, social media, and more. While each data point can provide valuable insights, too much information can obscure key trends and actionable insights. To combat this misconception, organizations should prioritize data relevance and clarity. Establishing clear objectives for data collection and analysis can help focus efforts on what truly matters. Instead of simply collecting data for the sake of it, teams should ask themselves: What questions are we trying to answer? What specific insights will drive our decision making? Employing data filtering techniques can also enhance the decision-making process. By honing in on the most relevant metrics and indicators, organizations can extract meaningful insights without being bogged down by excess information. Additionally, utilizing visualization tools can help present data in a more digestible format, allowing stakeholders to grasp key trends at a glance.

- **Misconception 3**: Data Analysis is Only for Experts: A widespread belief is that data analysis is an exclusive domain reserved for data scientists and analysts. This misconception can create barriers to entry for individuals and organizations seeking to leverage data in their decision-making processes. In reality, the ability to analyze data is becoming increasingly important for professionals across various fields, and numerous tools and resources exist to democratize data analysis. Many organizations may inadvertently foster a culture where only a select few are responsible for data analysis, leading to missed opportunities for insight generation. In doing so, they overlook the valuable perspectives that non-experts can contribute to data interpretation and decision making. To overcome this misconception, organizations should invest in data literacy initiatives that empower employees at all levels to engage with data. Training programs can provide foundational skills in data analysis, helping individuals understand how to interpret data and draw actionable insights. Additionally, user-friendly analytics tools are now widely available, enabling non-experts to explore data without requiring extensive technical expertise. Encouraging collaboration between data experts and non-experts can further enhance the analytical capabilities of an organization. By fostering a culture of shared knowledge and open communication, organizations can ensure that insights are derived from diverse viewpoints, ultimately leading to more well-rounded decision making.

- **Misconception 4:** Data Decisions Are Always Objective: Another misconception is that decisions based on data are inherently objective and free from bias. While data can provide a foundation for decision making, the interpretation of that data is influenced by human perspectives, experiences, and biases. Decision-makers may bring their own assumptions and preconceived notions to the analysis process, leading to subjective conclusions. This is particularly evident in situations where data is used to support pre-existing beliefs or agendas. For example, a marketing team may focus on data that supports their chosen strategy while ignoring data that suggests alternative approaches. This selective interpretation can lead to poor decision making and missed opportunities. To mitigate bias in data-driven decision making, organizations should implement practices that promote objectivity. Encouraging a culture of skepticism can help teams challenge assumptions and seek alternative explanations for observed data trends. Engaging diverse perspectives during the analysis process can also reduce the risk of bias; by incorporating input from individuals with different backgrounds and experiences, organizations can broaden their understanding of the data. Moreover, employing techniques such as blind analysis where analysts do not know the source of the data can help reduce bias in decision making. This practice allows for a more objective evaluation of the data, minimizing the influence of personal beliefs.

By recognizing that data does not equal truth, that more data is not always better, that data analysis is accessible to all, and that data decisions can be influenced by bias, organizations can cultivate a more nuanced understanding of the data landscape.

Promoting critical thinking, data literacy, and collaborative analysis will empower individuals and teams to harness the full potential of data. By fostering a culture of inquiry and openness, individuals and organizations can navigate the complexities of data-driven decision making, ultimately driving better outcomes and achieving their strategic objectives.

CHAPTER TWO

From Raw Numbers to Rich Narratives

In this dispensation effective communication becomes paramount with every passing day. Organizations are inundated with vast amounts of raw numbers and complex datasets, yet the ability to translate this information into compelling narratives is what ultimately drives understanding and action. The power of storytelling in data lies not only in its capacity to convey information but also in its potential to create emotional connections, foster engagement, and facilitate informed decision-making.

Storytelling is an ancient art form, woven into the fabric of human communication for millennia. From cave paintings to digital media, stories have served as a vehicle for sharing knowledge, preserving history, and conveying experiences. At its core, storytelling appeals to our innate desire for connection and understanding. In the context of data, storytelling transforms abstract numbers into relatable, tangible narratives that resonate with audiences. When data is presented without context or narrative, it risks being perceived as dry, impersonal, or even overwhelming. Consider a presentation filled with spreadsheets and charts devoid of any storyline; such an approach may leave audiences disengaged or confused. Conversely, when data is framed within a narrative, it becomes more accessible and engaging. A well-crafted story contextualizes the data, illuminating its relevance and implications, ultimately fostering a deeper understanding of the subject matter.

One of the primary benefits of storytelling in data presentation is its ability to provide context. Data points often represent specific moments in time or distinct aspects of a phenomenon, but without context, their significance can be obscured. By weaving data into a narrative, presenters can clarify the circumstances surrounding the numbers, thereby enhancing comprehension.

Let's consider a healthcare organization reporting a spike in patient readmission rates. Presenting the data alone such as the percentage increase might raise alarm but fail to convey the underlying reasons. However, if the data is contextualized within a narrative that explains changes in patient demographics, the introduction of new treatment protocols, or external factors affecting healthcare access, the audience gains a more nuanced understanding of the situation. This context not only clarifies the data but also allows stakeholders to engage in informed discussions about potential solutions.

Furthermore, storytelling can highlight trends and patterns that might otherwise go unnoticed in raw data. By framing data within a narrative arc beginning with a challenge, followed by actions taken, and concluding with results presenters can guide their audience through a logical progression that reveals insights and implications. This narrative structure not only aids comprehension but also helps audiences remember key takeaways long after the presentation is over.

Human beings are inherently emotional creatures, and stories resonate with us on a visceral level. Data alone may not evoke strong feelings; however, when coupled with storytelling, it can elicit empathy, motivation, and a sense of urgency. This emotional engagement is particularly important in areas such as healthcare, education, and social impact, where the stakes can be high. Emotional engagement can also inspire action. When stakeholders connect with the narrative presented alongside the data, they are more likely to feel motivated to contribute, advocate, or implement change. This phenomenon is evident in fundraising campaigns that share personal testimonials of individuals helped by donations. The combination of relatable stories and compelling data can create a powerful call to action that resonates with donors and drives them to support the cause.

To harness the power of storytelling in data, presenters must be intentional about how they craft their narratives. Several key elements contribute to an effective data narrative. One is clarity and simplicity. A successful data narrative begins with clarity. Presenters should aim to simplify complex data into digestible pieces. This might involve distilling large datasets into key takeaways, using straightforward language, and avoiding jargon that could alienate the audience.

A second element is structure and flow. Just as a traditional story follows a narrative arc which includes introduction, conflict, climax, resolution, data stories should have a clear structure. Presenters can start with a compelling introduction that sets the stage, outline the challenges or questions being addressed, present the data findings, and conclude with actionable insights or recommendations. Visualizations play a crucial role in data storytelling. Charts, graphs, and infographics can enhance understanding and retention by providing visual representations of data. Thoughtful visual design can draw attention to key points, highlight trends, and make the narrative more engaging. However, it's essential to ensure that visualizations complement the narrative rather than overwhelm it. Striking the right balance is essential.

To connect with the audience, these narratives should include relatable elements. This might involve using analogies, metaphors, or anecdotes that resonate with the audience's experiences or knowledge. Presenters should consider their audience's background and tailor their narrative accordingly, making it relevant and accessible. Finally, a compelling data narrative often concludes with a call to action. Presenters should articulate the implications of the data findings and encourage stakeholders to take specific steps or consider new perspectives. Whether it's advocating for a policy change, investing in a program, or simply raising awareness, a clear call to action can galvanize the audience toward meaningful engagement.

The power of storytelling in data cannot be overstated. As organizations grapple with increasing volumes of data, the ability to translate raw numbers into rich narratives is essential for effective communication. Storytelling enhances understanding by providing context, fostering emotional engagement, and highlighting key insights. By crafting compelling data narratives that prioritize clarity, structure, visual elements, relatability, and actionable outcomes, presenters can transform their data into a powerful tool for persuasion and influence.

What are the techniques for interpreting data and identifying key themes, and the process of crafting a narrative from both quantitative and qualitative data, and the tools and frameworks available to effectively visualize these data stories? By mastering these elements, an individual and firm can unlock the full potential of their data and communicate insights that inspire action.

The first step in transforming data into insightful stories is the interpretation of data itself. This process involves analyzing raw data to extract meaningful insights, trends, and patterns. To achieve this, data analysts must possess a deep understanding of the context and objectives of their analysis. The following strategies can help in interpreting data effectively. Before diving into the data, it's essential to establish clear objectives for the analysis. What questions are you trying to answer? What decisions will the insights inform? By having a clear purpose, analysts can focus their efforts on the most relevant data points and avoid getting lost in unnecessary details. After defining objectives, analysts should conduct exploratory data analysis

(EDA). EDA involves summarizing the main characteristics of the dataset, often using visual methods. This process helps analysts understand the data distribution, identify anomalies, and uncover initial trends. Techniques such as histograms, scatter plots, and box plots can provide valuable insights into the underlying patterns within the data.

In any dataset, certain metrics are more significant than others. Analysts must identify the key performance indicators (KPIs) that align with their objectives. For instance, a marketing team may focus on conversion rates, customer acquisition costs, and engagement metrics to assess campaign effectiveness. By concentrating on these essential metrics, analysts can tell a more focused and relevant story.

As analysts sift through the data, they should be vigilant for trends and patterns that emerge over time or across different groups. Are there seasonal fluctuations in sales? Do certain demographics respond differently to a marketing campaign? Recognizing these trends allows analysts to develop narratives that address the underlying causes and implications of the observed phenomena. Data does not exist in a vacuum; it is influenced by various external factors. Analysts must consider the broader context when interpreting data. Economic conditions, social trends, and industry changes can all impact the data. By contextualizing findings, analysts can provide a more comprehensive narrative that highlights the relevance and implications of the data.

Once analysts have interpreted the data and identified key themes, the next step is to craft a compelling narrative. A well-structured narrative not only conveys the findings but also guides the audience through the analysis, helping them understand the significance of the data. The following steps outline the process of crafting a narrative from data. Establish a clear structure. Just as a good story has a clear beginning, middle, and end, data narratives should follow a logical structure. The introduction should set the stage, outlining the problem or question being addressed. The middle section should present the data findings, including insights and trends, while the conclusion should summarize the implications and propose actionable recommendations.

The introduction is crucial for capturing the audience's attention. Presenters can start with a provocative question, a surprising statistic, or a relevant anecdote that relates to the data. This approach not only engages the audience but also provides a framework for understanding the subsequent analysis. Throughout the narrative, the information should be used strategically to support the key points being made. Presenters can highlight specific data points, trends, or comparisons that reinforce the overall message. Visualizations, such as charts and graphs, can help illustrate these points and make the data more digestible.

While quantitative data provides valuable insights, qualitative data such as interviews, testimonials, or open-ended survey responses can enrich the narrative. Qualitative insights add depth and context, allowing presenters to humanize the data and illustrate its real-world implications. For example, in a study on employee satisfaction, including quotes from employees can bring the data to life and highlight the personal experiences behind the numbers. As the narrative unfolds, it's essential to connect the data findings to broader implications. What do the insights mean for the organization or its stakeholders? How should decision-makers respond? By emphasizing the implications of the data, presenters can create a sense of urgency and relevance, motivating stakeholders to take action based on the insights provided.

Effective data visualization is a critical component of transforming data into insightful stories. Visualizations can enhance comprehension, highlight key trends, and make complex data more accessible. Several tools and frameworks are available to help organizations create impactful data visualizations:

- **Data Visualization Tools:** Numerous software tools and platforms can assist in creating visual representations of data. Popular options include Tableau, Power BI, and Google Data Studio. These tools enable users to create interactive dashboards, charts, and graphs that can be easily shared with stakeholders. When selecting a tool, organizations should consider factors such as ease of use, integration with existing data sources, and customization options.

- **Principles of Effective Visualization:** When creating visualizations, presenters should adhere to key principles that enhance clarity and impact. These principles include simplicity, consistency, context, and focus on key insights. Avoid clutter and focus on the most important data points. A clean and straightforward design allows the audience to grasp the message quickly. Use consistent colors, fonts, and styles across visualizations to create a cohesive narrative. This consistency helps the audience follow the story without confusion. Provide context for the visualizations by including labels, titles, and annotations. This information helps the audience interpret the data accurately. Highlight the most important insights within the visualizations. Use emphasis techniques, such as color or size variations, to draw attention to significant data points.

- **Storyboarding Visualizations:** Before creating visualizations, presenters can benefit from storyboarding their data narrative. This process involves sketching out the key visual elements that will accompany the narrative. By planning the visualizations alongside the narrative, presenters can ensure that each visualization supports the overall story and enhances understanding.

- **Interactive Visualizations:** In today's digital age, interactive visualizations are becoming increasingly popular. These allow users to explore data on their own terms, facilitating deeper engagement and understanding. Tools such as D3.js and Plotly enable the creation of interactive charts and graphs that can be embedded in presentations or websites. By allowing stakeholders to interact with the data, organizations can foster a more meaningful connection with the insights presented.

- **Feedback and Iteration:** Data visualization is not a one-time process; it requires feedback and iteration. Presenters should seek input from colleagues, stakeholders, or target audiences to refine their visualizations. By gathering feedback, organizations can identify areas for improvement and ensure that the visualizations effectively communicate the intended message.

It is essential to understand the strategies for making data relatable and engaging, the importance of understanding your audience, and the role of visuals, metaphors, and analogies in crafting impactful data narratives. By honing these techniques, communicators can ensure that their data-driven insights resonate with diverse audiences. The foundation of any successful data narrative lies in understanding the audience you are addressing. Different stakeholders have varied backgrounds, interests, and levels of familiarity with the subject matter, making it essential to tailor your narrative to meet their needs.

To begin, it's important to identify your audience. Are they executives, technical experts, or a general audience? Understanding their roles and responsibilities can help you gauge their level of expertise and interest in the topic. Once you've identified your audience, assess their prior knowledge of the subject. For example, a technical audience may be well-versed in specific data analytics concepts, while a general audience might require more foundational explanations. Adjusting your narrative accordingly is crucial; avoid overly complex jargon when addressing non-experts.

Next, consider the interests and pain points of your audience. What challenges do they face, and how can your data insights address those challenges? Framing your narrative around their needs enhances relevance and engagement. For instance, if you're presenting to a marketing team, focus on insights that relate to customer behavior and campaign performance. Furthermore, the language and tone of your narrative should reflect the audience's preferences. A formal tone may be suitable for a corporate board meeting, while a more conversational style might be appropriate for a community workshop. Using language that resonates with your audience fosters a connection and encourages engagement. Finally, consider soliciting feedback before finalizing your narrative. Seeking input from a small group of representatives from your target audience can provide valuable perspectives on clarity, relevance, and engagement, allowing you to refine your presentation.

Once you have a solid understanding of your audience, the next step is to make your data narrative relatable. Several strategies can help you achieve this goal. First, incorporate real-life examples. Using anecdotes or stories can bridge the gap between abstract data and relatable experiences. When audiences can see how data impacts individuals or communities, they are more likely to connect emotionally with the narrative.

Creating common ground with your audience can also enhance relatability. Start your narrative by acknowledging shared experiences or challenges related to the data. This approach fosters a sense of community and shared understanding, encouraging the audience to invest emotionally in the narrative. Simplicity is another key strategy. Complex data can alienate audiences if not presented clearly. Strive to simplify complex concepts by breaking them down into understandable components. Use straightforward language and avoid jargon when possible. A clear explanation of data findings makes them more accessible and engaging.

Utilizing analogies and metaphors is another effective way to make data relatable. By comparing complex data concepts to familiar situations, you can help the audience grasp the significance of the data more readily. For example, if you are explaining market volatility, you might compare it to a rollercoaster ride, emphasizing the ups and downs and the unpredictability inherent in both. Such comparisons not only make the data relatable but also evoke a sense of shared experience. Incorporating humor and emotion can significantly enhance engagement. Humor, when used appropriately, can be an effective way to connect with your audience. A well-placed joke or lighthearted comment can break the ice and create a relaxed atmosphere. Additionally, evoking emotion through storytelling can create a lasting impact. Sharing personal stories or poignant examples helps audiences connect with the data on a deeper level.

Visual elements play a critical role in engaging audiences with data narratives. Effective visuals can enhance understanding, highlight key points, and make data more accessible. To leverage visuals effectively, consider the following strategies.

First, choose the right visualization type. Different types of data lend themselves to different visualization formats. Consider the nature of the data when selecting a visualization type. For example, line charts are effective for showing trends over time, while bar charts work well for comparing discrete categories. Choosing the right format can enhance comprehension and engagement. Clarity should always be a top priority when designing visualizations. Avoid clutter and focus on presenting the most important information. Each visual should have a clear purpose and contribute to the overall narrative. Use legible fonts, contrasting colors, and straightforward labels to ensure that the audience can easily interpret the data.

Incorporating interactive elements into visualizations allows audiences to engage with the data on their own terms. Tools that enable users to explore data dynamically can foster a deeper connection and understanding.

Using infographics is another effective strategy. Infographics combine text and visuals to convey information succinctly and are particularly effective for summarizing key findings or processes. When presenting complex information, they can break it down into digestible pieces, making the narrative more engaging and easier to understand.

Finally, consider the flow of visualizations in your presentation. The sequence of visuals should follow the narrative flow, with each visual building on the previous one and guiding the audience through the story. Avoid presenting unrelated visuals that may confuse the audience or disrupt the narrative flow.

Metaphors and analogies as earlier mentioned can significantly enhance audience engagement by making complex data concepts more relatable and understandable. These literary devices create connections between the unfamiliar and the familiar, allowing audiences to grasp abstract ideas with ease. Begin by identifying the core themes or concepts you want to convey through your data narrative. What are the key takeaways you want your audience to understand? Once you have clarity on the themes, brainstorm metaphors or analogies that align with those ideas. Effective metaphors create connections between the data and experiences that resonate with the audience. For instance, when discussing market volatility, you might compare it to a rollercoaster ride, emphasizing the unpredictability involved. Such comparisons make the data relatable and evoke a sense of shared experience.

However, it's essential to be culturally sensitive when using metaphors and analogies. What may resonate with one group may not hold the same meaning for another. Ensure that your comparisons are culturally appropriate and widely understood by your audience to avoid confusion or misinterpretation. Keep metaphors simple and straightforward. Overly complex or convoluted metaphors may detract from the message rather than clarify it. Strive for clarity and simple comparisons, ensuring that the metaphor enhances understanding rather than complicates it. Finally, consider testing your metaphors and analogies with a small audience before delivering your narrative. Gathering feedback on whether the comparisons resonate and enhance understanding can help refine your narrative and ensure it effectively engages your target audience.

There are essential components of effective storytelling that can aid individuals weave compelling stories around data, drive engagement and achieve optimal results. At the heart are structure, emotional connection, and clarity. A well-structured story guides the audience through the data in a logical progression, helping them to grasp the significance of the insights being presented. Typically, a strong data narrative includes an introduction that sets the context, a body that explores the findings, and a conclusion that emphasizes the implications and encourages action.

Emotional connection is another critical element. Data, by itself, can often feel abstract and impersonal. However, when data is presented within a narrative framework that highlights real-world implications, it becomes more relatable. Personal stories, anecdotes, and examples can evoke emotions and foster a connection with the audience, making the data feel relevant to their lives. Clarity is equally vital in data storytelling. Presenters must ensure that the narrative is easy to follow and that the data is clearly represented. Using visuals, simplifying complex concepts, and avoiding jargon are all strategies that contribute to clarity. When the audience can easily understand the narrative, they are more likely to engage with the data and retain the insights being shared.

One compelling example of storytelling in data communication is the use of the "iceberg" analogy to illustrate the complexities of climate data. Climate scientists often present extensive datasets that reveal trends in temperature, sea level rise, and carbon emissions. However, the enormity of the data can overwhelm audiences, making it challenging to grasp the underlying issues. To address this, communicators have employed the iceberg analogy, which likens visible climate phenomena to the tip of an iceberg, while the larger, hidden issues lie beneath the surface. For instance, the rising global temperature may be visible in data visualizations, but the deeper implications such as the impact on biodiversity, extreme weather events, and socioeconomic factors remain obscured. By framing the climate crisis in this way, storytellers can create a powerful narrative that engages the audience. The iceberg analogy not only highlights the visible signs of climate change but also emphasizes the urgent need to address the underlying issues that contribute to these phenomena. This storytelling approach fosters a deeper understanding of the complexities of climate data, encouraging audiences to think critically about their role in addressing the crisis.

As organizations continue to navigate the complexities of this niche and its application, mastering the art of storytelling will be essential. By harnessing the power of narrative, data communicators can not only convey insights but also inspire action, ultimately driving positive change in their communities and beyond.

CHAPTER THREE

The Art of Asking the Right Questions

In the world of data science and analytics, the questions we ask are just as important as the data we analyze. The ability to formulate the right questions can significantly influence the quality of insights we gain and the decisions we make. This section delves into the art of asking the right questions, exploring how effective questioning can lead to better data-driven decisions, enhance problem-solving, and foster innovation.

For every successful data analysis lies a well-crafted question. Questions guide the analytical process, shaping the direction of research and the type of data collected. They serve as a compass, helping data scientists and decision-makers navigate through vast amounts of information to uncover meaningful insights. Without clear and purposeful questions, data analysis can become aimless, leading to confusion and misinterpretation.

Questions determine what data needs to be collected. For example, if a company wants to understand customer satisfaction, the specific questions posed will dictate whether they gather qualitative feedback from open-ended surveys or quantitative data from rating scales. By aligning data collection efforts with the right questions, organizations can ensure that the information they gather is relevant and actionable. Secondly, the nature of the questions posed influences the methods used for analysis. Descriptive questions may require statistical summaries, while exploratory questions may lead to more complex analyses involving regression or correlation. Furthermore, the way questions are framed can affect the interpretation of results. A question focused on "how many" may yield different insights than one framed as "why."

Ultimately, the right questions drive decision-making processes. By clarifying objectives and defining key metrics, organizations can make informed choices that align with their goals. Questions that encourage critical thinking and exploration foster a culture of inquiry, enabling teams to challenge assumptions and consider alternative perspectives.

To harness the power of questioning, it's essential to understand the characteristics that define effective questions. Here are some key attributes to consider. One is clarity. Effective questions should be clear and specific. Ambiguity can lead to misunderstandings and misinterpretations, resulting in ineffective analyses. For instance, a question like "What do customers think of our product?" is vague. In contrast, "What features of our product do customers find most valuable?" is more precise, directing the focus toward specific aspects.

Questions must be relevant to the goals and objectives of the analysis. They should align with the organization's mission and the specific problem at hand. Irrelevant questions can divert attention from critical issues and waste valuable resources. For example, a marketing team analyzing customer preferences should focus on questions related to consumer behavior rather than unrelated metrics like employee satisfaction. There should also be an element of processes that can yield action. Effective questions lead to actionable insights. They should be framed in a way that allows for practical solutions and informed decision-making. For instance, a question like "What factors contribute to customer churn?" invites analysis that can inform retention strategies, whereas a question that merely seeks to describe customer demographics may not yield direct action steps.

The choice between open-ended and closed-ended questions can significantly impact the depth of insights obtained. Open-ended questions encourage exploration and provide qualitative insights, while closed-ended questions yield quantitative data that is easier to analyze. Striking the right balance between the two types can enhance the richness of the analysis

Now what are the techniques for formulating these questions? Before crafting questions, it's crucial to define the problem statement clearly. Understanding the context and objectives of the analysis sets the foundation for meaningful questions. Engage stakeholders to gather insights about their concerns and priorities, ensuring that the questions resonate with their needs. The classic journalistic approach of asking "Who, What, When, Where, Why, and How" can be a valuable framework for generating questions. Each of these elements prompts specific inquiries that can uncover different dimensions of the issue. Examples include: Who are our target customers? What features do they value most? When do they typically make purchases? Where do they prefer to shop? Why do they choose our brand over competitors? How can we improve their experience?

The SMART criteria which stand for Specific, Measurable, Achievable, Relevant, and Time-bound can guide the formulation of effective questions. By ensuring that questions meet these criteria, analysts can enhance their clarity and focus. For example, instead of asking, "Is our marketing effective?" a SMART question would be, "What percentage of our targeted audience engaged with our latest campaign within the first month?" To foster creativity in question formulation, encourage divergent thinking. This approach involves brainstorming a wide range of questions without judgment or filtering. By generating a diverse set of inquiries, teams can identify unique angles and perspectives that may lead to innovative insights. Once the brainstorming session concludes, the team can refine the questions based on clarity, relevance, and action timeframes.

Question formulation is an iterative process. Encourage teams to revisit and refine their questions as new insights emerge. Regularly assess whether the questions continue to align with the analysis goals and adjust them accordingly. This flexibility allows for continuous improvement and ensures that the analysis remains focused on the most pressing issues.

The context in which questions are posed plays a significant role in shaping the analysis. Factors such as the industry, organizational culture, and specific challenges can influence the types of questions that are most relevant. Different industries may prioritize different questions based on their unique dynamics. Understanding the industry context helps analysts tailor their questions to address relevant challenges and opportunities. The culture of an organization also affects questioning practices. A culture that encourages curiosity and open dialogue fosters a collaborative environment for question formulation. Conversely, a more hierarchical culture may stifle innovative questioning and limit exploration. Leaders should cultivate an inclusive atmosphere where all team members feel empowered to contribute their perspectives and questions.

External factors, such as market trends, competitive dynamics, and emerging technologies, can shape the questions that need to be asked. Analysts should stay attuned to the broader context, recognizing that questions may need to evolve in response to changing circumstances. For instance, the COVID-19 pandemic prompted organizations to ask new questions about remote work, customer behavior shifts, and supply chain disruptions.

Despite the importance of effective questioning, several barriers can hinder the process. Recognizing and addressing these obstacles can enhance the quality of inquiry. Fear of judgment is an example of this barrier. Team members may hesitate to voice their questions due to fear of judgment or criticism. Creating a safe environment where all questions are valued encourages open dialogue and exploration. Leaders can model this behavior by openly asking questions themselves and acknowledging diverse perspectives. Cognitive biases can also influence the types of questions posed, leading to confirmation bias or anchoring effects. Analysts should strive to be aware of their biases and actively seek out alternative viewpoints. Encouraging a culture of curiosity and skepticism can help counteract these biases and promote critical thinking.

Unclear objectives or problem statements can lead to vague questioning. To mitigate this issue, teams should invest time in defining their goals and desired outcomes before formulating questions. This clarity will guide the questioning process and ensure that inquiries remain focused and relevant.

The art of asking the right questions is a crucial skill for making relevant and effective decisions every day. Effective questions guide the analytical process, shape data collection, and drive meaningful insights. By understanding the characteristics of effective questions, employing techniques for formulation, and considering the context in which they are posed, individuals and organizations can enhance their data analysis capabilities.

CHAPTER FOUR

Patterns And Predictions: Finding Clarity in Chaos

In the vast sea of information that defines our current age, the ability to discern patterns from data has become a pivotal skill across various fields. As organizations and individuals increasingly rely on accurate insights, understanding patterns becomes essential for making informed decisions. Patterns in data can reveal underlying trends, correlations, and anomalies that inform strategies, predict future outcomes, and enhance operational efficiencies. Here we will delve into the nature of patterns in data, the types of patterns we can identify, the significance of recognizing these patterns, and the techniques used to uncover them.

A pattern in data is a recurring sequence or arrangement of elements that exhibits regularity. This can manifest as a trend that indicates a general direction over time, a cycle that shows periodic fluctuations, or an anomaly that stands out as an outlier from expected behavior. Patterns emerge when data points are collected and analyzed, revealing structures that may not be apparent in isolated observations.

Recognizing patterns is not merely an academic exercise; it is a practical necessity for effective decision-making. In a business context, for instance, identifying customer purchasing patterns can lead to improved marketing strategies, inventory management, and customer relationship management. In healthcare, recognizing patterns in patient data can enhance diagnostic accuracy and treatment plans. The implications of pattern recognition are vast and impact various sectors, from finance to education, logistics to public policy. Patterns are often driven by underlying phenomena or variables. For example, economic data may exhibit patterns due to market forces such as supply and demand, consumer behavior, or regulatory changes. In the natural sciences, patterns can emerge from biological processes, environmental changes, or physical laws. By understanding the context in which data is generated, analysts can better interpret the patterns that arise, leading to more accurate insights.

They can be categorized into several types, each providing different insights and implications. Understanding these types is crucial for effective analysis.

- **Trends:** Trends represent a general direction in which data points move over time. They can be upward, downward, or flat, indicating increases, decreases, or stability in the variable of interest. For example, a consistent increase in sales over several quarters may indicate a positive trend that businesses can capitalize on. Identifying trends is critical for long-term strategic planning, as they often inform forecasts and help organizations allocate resources effectively.

- **Cycles:** This refers to patterns that repeat over a specific period. Unlike trends, which may indicate a one-way movement, cycles exhibit fluctuations that occur at regular intervals. A classic example of cyclical patterns is seasonal sales variations, where retail sales may spike during holidays and decline afterward. Understanding cycles is essential for businesses to anticipate fluctuations and adapt their strategies accordingly.

- **Anomalies:** Anomalies, or outliers, are data points that deviate significantly from the expected pattern. Identifying anomalies is crucial as they can indicate critical insights or issues that require attention. For instance, a sudden spike in web traffic may signal a successful marketing campaign or, conversely, a potential security breach. Anomalies can also indicate errors in data collection or processing, making it essential to investigate their causes thoroughly.

- **Correlations:** These patterns reveal relationships between two or more variables. For instance, a positive correlation indicates that as one variable increases, the other also tends to increase, while a negative correlation suggests that one variable decreases as the other increases. Understanding correlations can help analysts identify dependencies and relationships within data, guiding decision-making processes.

- **Clusters:** Clustering patterns emerge when data points group together based on similarities or common characteristics. Clustering is often used in customer segmentation, where businesses group customers with similar behaviors or preferences to tailor marketing efforts. Identifying clusters can uncover hidden segments in the data that may warrant specialized strategies.

- **Spatial Patterns:** In geographic data, spatial patterns illustrate the distribution of data points across geographical areas. These patterns can reveal regional trends, such as population density, disease spread, or resource allocation. Spatial analysis is crucial for urban planning, environmental monitoring, and public health initiatives.

Recognizing patterns in data is not just an intellectual exercise; it is a fundamental driver of effective decision-making and strategic planning. The significance of pattern recognition can be summarized in several important ways.

Understanding patterns allow organizations to make data-driven decisions rather than relying on intuition or guesswork. They serve as the foundation for forecasting future outcomes. By analyzing historical patterns, organizations can build predictive models that anticipate future trends and behaviors. This capability is particularly valuable in industries like finance, where accurate predictions can significantly impact investment strategies.

Patterns can reveal opportunities for growth or potential threats to an organization. For example, a sudden increase in customer complaints may indicate an emerging issue that needs immediate attention, while a pattern of positive customer feedback may highlight areas for expansion or new product development. It enables organizations to allocate resources more effectively. If a company that identifies seasonal sales patterns can optimize inventory management and staffing levels, reducing costs and improving service levels. Identifying patterns can lead to process improvements and enhanced operational efficiency. For example, analyzing production data may reveal bottlenecks or inefficiencies, allowing organizations to streamline processes and reduce waste. They can also inform long-term strategic planning by providing insights into market dynamics and consumer behavior. By recognizing emerging trends, organizations can position themselves for success in an ever-changing environment.

With the importance of recognizing patterns established, it is essential to explore the techniques and tools available for identifying patterns in data. Analysts, individuals and data scientists can employ a variety of methods to uncover patterns, depending on the nature of the data and the questions being asked.

Statistical methods, such as regression analysis and hypothesis testing, are fundamental techniques for identifying patterns. Regression analysis, for example, allows analysts to quantify the relationship between variables and assess the strength of those relationships. By analyzing correlations, analysts can uncover trends and associations within the data. Visual representations of data are powerful tools for identifying patterns. Graphs, charts, and heat maps can reveal trends and anomalies that may not be apparent in raw data. Visualization tools allow analysts to explore data intuitively, facilitating pattern recognition through visual cues. Time series analysis focuses on data points collected over time, enabling analysts to identify trends, cycles, and seasonality. Techniques such as moving averages and exponential smoothing can help smooth out noise in the data, making it easier to discern underlying patterns.

Machine learning algorithms are increasingly used to identify patterns in large and complex datasets. Supervised learning techniques, such as decision trees and neural networks, can be trained to recognize patterns based on labeled data. Unsupervised learning methods, such as clustering and association analysis, can uncover patterns in unlabeled data without predefined categories.

Data mining involves extracting valuable insights from large datasets using various techniques, including pattern recognition and anomaly detection. Data mining tools can analyze vast amounts of information to identify hidden patterns and trends that may not be readily apparent.

Exploratory Data Analysis (EDA) is another technique that can be employed. It is a crucial step in the data analysis process that involves examining datasets to summarize their main characteristics and identify patterns. Techniques such as summary statistics, data visualization, and correlation analysis are employed during the process to gain insights into the data's structure. Understanding the context and domain from which the data originates is essential for effective pattern recognition. Analysts who possess domain knowledge can more easily identify relevant patterns and interpret their significance within the specific context. This expertise allows for a deeper understanding of the factors influencing the data.

Patterns reveal insights that guide strategic planning, inform resource allocation, and enhance operational efficiency. By recognizing different types of patterns, analysts can leverage statistical methods, data visualization, machine learning, and domain knowledge to uncover meaningful insights from complex datasets.

Predictions in Data Science

The role of predictions in data science is paramount and has emerged as a transformative capability for organizations. Predictions allow businesses to anticipate future trends, optimize operations, and make informed decisions that can lead to enhanced performance and competitiveness. We will explore the role of predictive analytics in data science, the methodologies employed for making predictions, the significance of predictive insights, and the challenges faced in this dynamic field.

Predictive analytics is a branch of data analytics that focuses on using statistical algorithms and machine learning techniques to identify the likelihood of future outcomes based on historical data. By analyzing patterns and trends within data, organizations can build models that provide insights into what may happen in the future. These insights can be invaluable for decision-making, enabling organizations to act proactively rather than reactively.

The process of predictive analytics generally involves several core steps namely data collection, data preparation, feature selection, model building, model evaluation, deployment, monitoring and maintenance.

The foundation of predictive analytics is data. Organizations must gather relevant data from various sources, which can include transaction records, customer interactions, social media activity, and sensor data. The quality and comprehensiveness of the data are crucial, as they directly influence the accuracy of predictions. Once data is collected, it often requires cleaning and preparation. This process involves removing duplicates, addressing missing values, and transforming data into a format suitable for analysis. Proper data preparation is essential for building reliable predictive models. In predictive modeling, features are the individual measurable properties or characteristics of the data. Identifying the right features to include in a model is critical, as irrelevant or redundant features can lead to overfitting and decreased predictive performance.

Various statistical and machine learning algorithms are employed to create predictive models. Common techniques include regression analysis, decision trees, random forests, and neural networks. The choice of algorithm depends on the nature of the data and the specific predictive task at hand. Once a predictive model is built, it must be evaluated for its accuracy and reliability. This is typically done using metrics such as mean absolute error, root mean squared error, and accuracy scores. Cross-validation techniques are often employed to ensure that the model performs well on unseen data.

After evaluation, the predictive model is deployed for use in real and every day applications. This may involve integrating the model into existing systems or creating user-friendly dashboards that allow stakeholders to access and interpret predictions easily. Predictive models require ongoing monitoring and maintenance to ensure their continued accuracy. As new data becomes available or as underlying patterns change, models may need to be retrained or updated to maintain their effectiveness.

Several methodologies are commonly employed in predictive analytics, each with its strengths and weaknesses. Understanding these methodologies is essential for selecting the most appropriate approach for specific predictive tasks. Regression analysis is one of the most widely used predictive modeling techniques. It examines the relationship between dependent and independent variables, allowing analysts to make predictions based on input features. Linear regression, for example, predicts a continuous outcome based on the linear relationship between variables, while logistic regression is used for binary outcomes.

Time series forecasting is specifically designed for predicting future values based on previously observed values over time. This methodology is commonly used in finance, economics, and inventory management. Techniques such as ARIMA (AutoRegressive Integrated Moving Average) and exponential smoothing are popular choices for time series analysis.

Machine learning encompasses a wide range of algorithms that can be employed for predictive analytics. These include supervised learning techniques, such as decision trees and support vector machines, which learn from labeled training data, and unsupervised learning methods, such as clustering algorithms, which identify patterns in unlabeled data.

Neural networks, particularly deep learning models, have gained significant popularity in recent years for their ability to handle complex and high-dimensional data. These models consist of interconnected nodes (neurons) that can learn hierarchical representations of data, making them effective for tasks such as image recognition, natural language processing, and more. Ensemble methods combine multiple predictive models to improve overall performance. Techniques such as bagging (e.g., Random Forests) and boosting (e.g., Gradient Boosting Machines) leverage the strengths of individual models while mitigating their weaknesses. This approach often results in more robust predictions. Finally, is the use of Natural Language Processing (NLP) method. This technique enable organizations to analyze and predict outcomes based on textual data. Sentiment analysis, for instance, can provide insights into customer opinions and sentiments, helping businesses anticipate market trends and consumer behavior.

The ability to generate predictive insights has profound implications for organizations across various sectors. Here are some key areas where predictive analytics plays a critical role.

These insights empower organizations to make decisions that are grounded in evidence rather than intuition. By understanding potential future outcomes, decision-makers can weigh options more effectively and choose courses of action that align with their strategic goals. Predictive analytics enables organizations to identify and mitigate risks proactively.

Institutions can use predictive analytics to optimize resource allocation. In manufacturing, predictive maintenance models can anticipate equipment failures, allowing for timely repairs and reducing downtime.

Predictive analytics helps organizations tailor their products and services to meet customer preferences. By analyzing customer behavior patterns, businesses can anticipate needs, personalize marketing efforts, and improve overall customer satisfaction. Businesses can leverage these analytics to inform long-term strategic planning. By understanding emerging trends and potential market shifts, businesses can adapt their strategies to remain competitive. This foresight can be particularly valuable in industries characterized by rapid change, such as technology and consumer goods. By anticipating future events and behaviors, organizations can achieve significant cost savings and efficiency gains. Predictive analytics can streamline operations, reduce waste, and enhance productivity, ultimately contributing to improved profitability.

As much as there are many advantages, predictive analytics is not without its challenges. Organizations must navigate several obstacles to effectively harness the power of predictive insights: The accuracy of predictive models hinges on the quality of the data used. Incomplete, inconsistent, or biased data can lead to unreliable predictions. Organizations must invest in robust data management practices to ensure data quality and accessibility.

As predictive models become more sophisticated, they may also become more complex and challenging to interpret. This complexity can create barriers to understanding predictions, especially for non-technical stakeholders. Balancing model accuracy with interpretability is a critical consideration. These models can suffer from overfitting, where the model becomes too tailored to the training data and fails to generalize to new data. Conversely, underfitting occurs when a model is too simplistic to capture the underlying patterns. Finding the right balance is essential for building effective predictive models. Predictive models rely on historical data, but if underlying patterns change over time due to shifts in consumer behavior, market conditions, or external factors the accuracy of predictions can diminish. Organizations must continuously monitor and update their models to ensure they remain relevant.

The use of the analytics raises ethical concerns, particularly around issues of privacy and bias. Organizations must be mindful of how they collect, store, and use data, ensuring that they adhere to ethical standards and regulatory requirements. For it to be truly impactful, organizations must integrate predictive insights into their decision-making processes. This requires a cultural shift that emphasizes data-driven decision-making and collaboration between data scientists and business stakeholders.

As predictive analytics continues to evolve, its impact across diverse industries has become increasingly evident. The ability to leverage these insights not only enhances operational efficiency but also drives strategic decision-making and innovation. In the healthcare sector, predictive analytics has emerged as a game-changer, enabling providers to enhance patient care, optimize operations, and reduce costs. Healthcare providers are increasingly using predictive models to identify patients at high risk for adverse events, such as hospital readmissions or disease progression. By analyzing historical patient data, including demographics, medical history, and treatment outcomes, providers can intervene proactively, tailoring care plans to individual needs.

Predictive analytics allows organizations to analyze trends within specific populations, helping to identify health risks and disparities. By understanding these patterns, public health officials can implement targeted interventions, allocate resources more effectively, and improve health outcomes across communities.

Hospitals and clinics can utilize predictive insights to optimize scheduling, staffing, and resource allocation. By forecasting patient volumes based on historical data, healthcare facilities can better manage capacity, reduce wait times, and enhance overall patient satisfaction. It can also support clinical decision-making by providing evidence-based recommendations at the point of care. For instance, predictive models can alert healthcare providers to potential complications based on patient data, facilitating timely interventions and improving treatment efficacy.

The finance industry is another sector where predictive analytics plays a crucial role, particularly in risk management and fraud detection. Financial institutions rely on predictive insights to make informed decisions and mitigate risks associated with lending, investments, and transactions. Predictive models are commonly used to assess the creditworthiness of borrowers. By analyzing historical data, including credit history, income, and employment status, lenders can predict the likelihood of default. This enables financial institutions to make informed lending decisions and set appropriate interest rates. It helps financial institutions identify and prevent fraudulent activities by analyzing transaction patterns and flagging anomalies. Machine learning algorithms can learn from historical fraud cases, allowing organizations to develop models that detect suspicious behavior in real time.

It is essential for organizations to embrace predictive analytics as a core component of their operations. By investing in data management, analytics capabilities, and talent development, organizations can unlock the full potential of predictive insights and position themselves for success in an increasingly fast paced world. In doing so, they can not only navigate the complexities of their respective industries but also drive innovation and create value for stakeholders.

While predictive analytics offers significant advantages across various industries, it is not without its challenges and ethical considerations. As organizations increasingly rely on data-driven insights, they must navigate complexities related to data quality, model accuracy, privacy, and ethical implications.

One of the foremost challenges in predictive analytics is ensuring data quality and availability. Predictive models depend heavily on the data used for training and validation. Poor data quality can lead to inaccurate predictions, ultimately undermining the effectiveness of analytical efforts. In many cases, organizations struggle with incomplete datasets. Missing values can distort the results of predictive models, leading to biased outcomes. To mitigate this, organizations must invest in comprehensive data collection methods and robust data management practices. This includes defining clear protocols for data entry, ensuring consistency, and implementing mechanisms for regular data audits.

Inconsistencies in data formats, terminology, and coding can create significant challenges in predictive analytics. When data is sourced from multiple systems or departments, discrepancies can arise, affecting the integrity of the analysis. Standardizing data formats and establishing clear data governance policies can help ensure consistency and facilitate accurate predictive modeling. Inaccurate data can stem from human error, outdated information, or biased collection methods. Organizations must prioritize data validation processes to identify and rectify inaccuracies before they impact predictive models. Employing automated data cleaning tools can enhance data accuracy and reliability. Predictive models often rely on historical data to make forecasts about future events. If the data is outdated, predictions may become irrelevant. Organizations should implement strategies to ensure that data is regularly updated and that predictive models are recalibrated to reflect the most current information available.

As change occurs, these models have become increasingly complex, particularly with the rise of machine learning and deep learning techniques. While these advanced models can yield highly accurate predictions, their complexity can present challenges.

A critical concern in predictive modeling is the balance between overfitting and underfitting. Overfitting occurs when a model becomes too tailored to the training data, capturing noise rather than underlying patterns. Conversely, underfitting happens when a model is too simplistic to capture the complexities of the data. Striking the right balance is essential for developing effective predictive models. Complex models, especially those involving deep learning, can often function as "black boxes," making it difficult for stakeholders to understand how predictions are generated. This lack of interpretability can hinder trust in the model and its outputs. Organizations must prioritize model transparency and develop techniques for explaining predictions to non-technical stakeholders, thereby facilitating informed decision-making. Choosing appropriate metrics to evaluate model performance is crucial. Organizations must ensure that they select metrics that align with their specific objectives and use cases. A focus solely on accuracy may overlook other critical aspects, such as precision, recall, and F1 score. Establishing a comprehensive evaluation framework can help organizations gauge model effectiveness more holistically.

There are ethical considerations surrounding data usage and model implementation which have become paramount. The potential for bias, privacy violations, and unintended consequences must be carefully addressed.

Predictive models can inadvertently perpetuate bias present in historical data. For instance, if training data reflects societal biases, the resulting model may reinforce these biases, leading to discriminatory outcomes. Organizations must implement practices to identify and mitigate bias throughout the data collection, modeling, and evaluation processes. This includes conducting fairness audits, employing bias detection tools, and ensuring diverse representation in training datasets.

The collection and analysis of personal data raise significant privacy concerns. Organizations must navigate legal and ethical frameworks surrounding data privacy, including regulations like GDPR and CCPA. It is essential to obtain informed consent from individuals whose data is being used and to ensure that data is anonymized or pseudonymized wherever possible. Developing clear data governance policies can help organizations protect individual privacy while utilizing predictive analytics effectively. As predictive analytics increasingly informs critical decisions, the question of accountability arises. Organizations must establish clear lines of responsibility for the outcomes produced by predictive models. This includes ensuring that decision-makers understand the limitations of the models and are aware of the potential consequences of their use. Regular audits and reviews of model performance can help organizations maintain accountability and address any issues that may arise.

Transparency in predictive analytics processes is vital for building trust among stakeholders. Organizations should communicate openly about how data is collected, how models are built, and the factors influencing predictions. Providing stakeholders with access to model outputs, evaluation metrics, and explanations of how predictions are generated can foster trust and engagement.

Implementing predictive analytics solutions and integrating them into existing business processes can pose significant challenges for organizations. Successful integration requires careful planning, collaboration, and change management.

First, organizations may encounter resistance from employees who are accustomed to traditional decision-making processes. Promoting a data-driven culture that emphasizes the value of predictive analytics is essential for overcoming this resistance. Training programs, workshops, and success stories can help demonstrate the benefits of predictive insights and encourage adoption. Effective predictive analytics requires collaboration between data scientists, domain experts, and business stakeholders. Bridging the gap between technical and non-technical teams is crucial for ensuring that predictive models align with organizational objectives and real-world applications. Institutions should foster a collaborative environment that encourages knowledge sharing and cross-functional teamwork.

As organizations grow and evolve, their predictive analytics capabilities must scale accordingly. Implementing flexible solutions that can adapt to changing data landscapes and business needs is critical. Organizations should consider cloud-based analytics platforms and modular solutions that can easily integrate with existing systems. Predictive analytics is not a one-time effort but an ongoing process that requires continuous monitoring, evaluation, and improvement. Organizations should establish mechanisms for regularly reviewing model performance, updating algorithms, and incorporating new data sources. Creating a culture of continuous improvement will enhance the effectiveness of predictive analytics initiatives.

CHAPTER FIVE

Bias And Belief: The Hidden Influences on Decision Making

Cognitive biases are systematic patterns of deviation from norm or rationality in judgment, often leading individuals to make illogical or irrational decisions. These biases are inherent in human thinking and can significantly influence our perceptions, behaviors, and decision-making processes. Understanding cognitive biases is crucial for anyone seeking to make better decisions, whether in personal life, business, or public policy.

These biases stem from the brain's attempt to simplify information processing. Given the vast amount of information we encounter daily, our brains use mental shortcuts, or heuristics, to navigate complex decisions. While these shortcuts can be helpful, they often lead to errors in judgment. Cognitive biases can be classified into several categories, including decision making, social, and memory biases. Decision-making biases directly affect our choices and include confirmation bias, anchoring bias, and overconfidence bias. Social biases are biases which influence how we perceive others and ourselves, such as in-group bias and stereotyping. Memory biases affect how we recall past events, including hindsight bias and the availability heuristic. Understanding these categories allows us to recognize their prevalence in everyday decision-making scenarios.

There are various types of cognitive biases. Confirmation bias is the tendency to search for, interpret, and remember information in a way that confirms one's preexisting beliefs or hypotheses. For example, a person who believes in a particular political ideology may only seek out news sources that align with their views, disregarding opposing viewpoints. This bias can lead to polarized thinking and an inability to engage in constructive dialogue. Anchoring bias occurs when individuals rely too heavily on the first piece of information they encounter (the "anchor") when making decisions. For instance, if someone is presented with a high initial price for a product, subsequent prices may seem reasonable by comparison, even if they are still inflated. Anchoring can distort our perception of value and lead to poor purchasing decisions.

In overconfidence bias, many individuals tend to overestimate their knowledge, skills, or accuracy in predictions, leading to excessive risk-taking and poor decision-making. This bias can be particularly dangerous in fields such as finance or project management, where overconfidence can lead to significant losses or project failures. Availability heuristic refers to the tendency to rely on immediate examples that come to mind when evaluating a specific topic or decision. If recent news reports highlight a particular type of crime, individuals may overestimate the prevalence of that crime, leading to fear and misguided policy responses. Hindsight bias often referred to as the "knew-it-all-along" effect, is the inclination to see events as having been predictable after they have already occurred. This bias can distort our understanding of past decisions and hinder learning from experience.

Cognitive biases arise from the interplay of various psychological mechanisms that shape how we process information. Several key factors contribute to the development of these biases. Heuristics are mental shortcuts that simplify decision-making processes. While they can be efficient, they often lead to oversimplification and misjudgments. The reliance on heuristics is a fundamental aspect of human cognition, allowing individuals to make quick decisions in uncertain situations. Emotions play a significant role in decision-making. Positive or negative emotions can cloud judgment and lead to biased conclusions. For instance, fear can amplify the availability heuristic, causing individuals to overemphasize recent traumatic events when evaluating risk.

Social dynamics, including groupthink and peer pressure, can exacerbate cognitive biases. In group settings, individuals may conform to the dominant opinion, suppressing dissenting views and leading to poor collective decisions. This psychological phenomenon occurs when individuals experience discomfort due to conflicting beliefs or attitudes. To alleviate this discomfort, individuals may adjust their beliefs or perceptions, leading to biases in judgment.

The influence of these biases on decision-making is profound and far-reaching. In both personal and professional contexts, they can lead to suboptimal choices and unintended consequences. It affects everyday decisions, from financial choices to relationship dynamics. For example, confirmation bias can lead individuals to overlook red flags in a partner's behavior, while overconfidence bias may cause someone to make poor financial investments based on inflated self-assessments. In the corporate world, cognitive biases can impact strategic decision-making and organizational culture. Leadership teams that fall victim to groupthink may make poor choices that stifle innovation and adaptability. Additionally, biases in hiring processes can lead to a lack of diversity and missed opportunities for growth. Policymakers must navigate cognitive biases when crafting legislation and addressing societal issues. Availability heuristics may lead to disproportionate responses to rare events, such as implementing stringent regulations following a high-profile incident. Furthermore, confirmation bias can hinder policymakers' ability to consider alternative viewpoints and adapt policies based on new evidence.

Recognizing the existence of cognitive biases is the first step toward mitigating their effects. Several strategies can be employed to reduce bias in decision-making such as educating individuals and teams about common cognitive biases is crucial for fostering awareness. Workshops and training sessions can help participants identify biases in their thinking and develop strategies to counteract them.

Implementing structured decision-making frameworks can help minimize the influence of biases. Tools such as decision trees, checklists, and multi-criteria analysis provide systematic approaches to evaluate options, reducing reliance on gut feelings. Encouraging diverse viewpoints within teams can combat groupthink and promote critical thinking. Actively seeking dissenting opinions and engaging in constructive debate can lead to more robust decision-making processes. Establishing feedback loops allows individuals to learn from past decisions and refine their approaches. By reflecting on outcomes and identifying biases that influenced decisions, individuals can improve their decision-making over time.

They are pervasive and can have a profound impact on decision-making. Understanding how to identify and mitigate these biases is crucial for enhancing our judgment and making informed choices. We will explore effective strategies for recognizing personal biases and beliefs, structured decision-making frameworks that can help reduce bias, and the role of data literacy in promoting objective analysis.

The first step in mitigating cognitive biases is to develop self-awareness. Individuals must learn to recognize their biases and understand how these biases can influence their decision-making processes. This involves introspection and a willingness to question one's own thoughts and beliefs. There are several strategies for enhancing self-awareness and recognizing personal biases. Engaging in reflective practices, such as journaling or meditation, can help individuals gain insights into their thought processes. By regularly reflecting on decisions and the factors influencing them, individuals can identify patterns of thinking that may indicate bias. For example, after making a significant decision, a person can review the reasoning behind their choice and consider whether any biases may have played a role.

Seeking feedback from others can provide valuable perspectives on one's decision-making. Engaging colleagues, mentors, or friends in discussions about choices can help uncover biases that may not be immediately apparent. Constructive criticism can illuminate blind spots and encourage individuals to reconsider their assumptions. Familiarizing oneself with common cognitive biases is essential for recognizing them in real-time. Biases such as confirmation bias, anchoring bias, and overconfidence bias can manifest in various situations. By understanding these biases and their potential effects, individuals can become more vigilant in identifying them in their own thought processes. Practicing mindfulness can enhance awareness of thoughts and emotions as they arise. Mindfulness encourages individuals to observe their cognitive processes without judgment, creating space for critical thinking. This practice can help individuals notice when their emotions or preconceived beliefs may be influencing their decisions.

Structured decision-making frameworks are systematic approaches that guide individuals through the decision-making process. These frameworks help mitigate cognitive biases by providing a clear structure for evaluating options, considering alternatives, and weighing the potential outcomes. Several effective frameworks can be employed.

Decision trees are visual representations of decisions and their potential consequences. They help individuals map out choices and evaluate the possible outcomes of each option. By laying out the decision-making process in a structured manner, individuals can make more informed choices and reduce reliance on gut feelings. Cost-benefit analysis involves comparing the expected costs and benefits of different options. This framework encourages individuals to quantify their choices, making it easier to identify the most favorable outcomes. By focusing on measurable factors, individuals can mitigate emotional biases that may cloud their judgment. Multi-Criteria decision analysis (MCDA) is a structured approach that evaluates multiple conflicting criteria in decision-making. This method allows individuals to assess various factors, prioritize them according to their importance, and arrive at a well-informed decision. By incorporating diverse criteria, individuals can avoid overemphasis on any single aspect of the decision.

SWOT analysis (Strengths, Weaknesses, Opportunities, Threats) is a strategic planning tool that helps individuals and organizations evaluate a situation comprehensively. By identifying internal strengths and weaknesses, as well as external opportunities and threats, individuals can gain a holistic understanding of the context surrounding their decisions. This comprehensive perspective can counteract biases by prompting consideration of multiple factors. Collaborative decision-making can reduce biases through diverse perspectives. Techniques such as brainstorming, nominal group technique, or Delphi method encourage participation from multiple stakeholders. By incorporating a range of viewpoints, groups can counteract individual biases and enhance the quality of their decisions.

Data literacy is the ability to read, understand, create, and communicate data effectively. In this current dispensation, enhancing data literacy is crucial for mitigating biases and improving decision-making processes. Here's how data literacy can play a significant role. It equips individuals with the skills to critically evaluate data sources, methodologies, and interpretations. Understanding how data is collected and analyzed can help individuals recognize potential biases in data reporting. This awareness is essential for making informed decisions based on reliable information.

Individuals with strong data literacy can leverage data to support their decision-making processes. By relying on empirical evidence rather than personal beliefs or assumptions, individuals can enhance objectivity in their choices. Data-driven decision-making promotes a culture of accountability and transparency. Effective data visualization is a key component of data literacy. Visualizations can simplify complex data and reveal patterns that may not be apparent in raw numbers. By understanding how to create and interpret visualizations, individuals can enhance their comprehension of data and reduce the influence of cognitive biases.

A basic understanding of statistics can empower individuals to evaluate the significance of data and avoid common pitfalls, such as misinterpreting correlation as causation. Knowledge of statistical concepts helps individuals critically assess data claims and make informed decisions based on sound reasoning. Organizations that prioritize data literacy create an environment where data is valued in decision-making. Training programs, workshops, and access to data resources can empower employees to utilize data effectively. A data-driven culture fosters informed decision-making at all levels and helps mitigate the influence of personal biases.

Creating a culture of bias awareness within organizations is essential for promoting effective decision-making. Institutions should prioritize initiatives that foster awareness of cognitive biases and encourage critical thinking. There are several strategies for building such a culture. This includes training, workshops, encouraging open dialogue, leadership commitment, performance evaluation and feedback mechanisms.

In our exploration of cognitive biases and beliefs, it becomes increasingly clear that awareness and proactive measures are essential in fostering better decision-making. We will discuss practical strategies for developing bias awareness, enhancing critical thinking, and promoting a culture of informed decision-making. By incorporating these strategies into daily practices, individuals and organizations can significantly improve their decision-making processes. Continuous learning is a cornerstone of effective decision-making. The rapidly changing landscape of knowledge and information necessitates that individuals remain open to new ideas and willing to adapt their mental models. Continuous learning encourages individuals to challenge their beliefs and biases, fostering a mindset of curiosity and adaptability.

Organizations should cultivate a culture that values lifelong learning. This can be achieved by offering professional development opportunities, such as workshops, online courses, and mentorship programs. By investing in employees' education, organizations empower them to think critically and approach decisions with a broader perspective.

Creating platforms for knowledge sharing within organizations can facilitate continuous learning. This can include regular team meetings, discussion forums, or collaborative projects where individuals can exchange ideas and insights. Such environments encourage employees to engage with diverse viewpoints and challenge their own assumptions. Encouraging reflective practices among individuals can enhance self-awareness and promote learning from past experiences. Regularly reflecting on decisions, successes, and failures can provide valuable insights into how biases may have influenced outcomes. Journaling, peer discussions, or supervision sessions can facilitate this reflective process.

Critical thinking is essential for recognizing and mitigating biases in decision-making. By honing critical thinking skills, individuals can approach decisions more analytically and thoughtfully. Organizations should incorporate critical thinking training into their development programs. This can involve workshops that focus on evaluating evidence, recognizing assumptions, and analyzing arguments. By providing employees with the tools to think critically, organizations can promote a more objective decision-making process.

Fostering a culture that encourages questioning can enhance critical thinking. Employees should feel empowered to ask challenging questions, seek clarification, and express dissenting opinions. Creating an environment where inquiry is valued can stimulate deeper discussions and lead to better-informed decisions. Scenario-based learning and simulations can provide practical experiences that enhance critical thinking. By engaging in role-playing exercises or analyzing hypothetical situations, individuals can practice decision-making in a safe environment. This experiential learning can help individuals recognize biases and improve their analytical skills.

Diversity in teams is a powerful antidote to cognitive biases. Diverse perspectives can challenge groupthink and foster more robust decision-making processes. Institutions should prioritize diversity and inclusion in their hiring practices. By bringing together individuals from different backgrounds, experiences, and viewpoints, organizations can create teams that are better equipped to tackle complex problems. Diversity can enhance creativity, innovation, and critical evaluation of ideas.

Facilitating cross-functional collaboration can expose individuals to different perspectives and expertise. By working with colleagues from various departments, team members can broaden their understanding of issues and consider diverse viewpoints in their decision-making processes. Establishing advisory groups with diverse representation can provide valuable insights into decision-making. These groups can offer guidance on policies, practices, and strategies, ensuring that decisions are informed by a range of perspectives. By actively seeking input from diverse stakeholders, organizations can mitigate the effects of biases.

Structured decision-making frameworks provide systematic approaches that help individuals navigate complex decisions while minimizing the influence of biases. Decision-making frameworks that emphasize data-driven analysis can reduce reliance on intuition and gut feelings. By using empirical evidence to guide decisions, individuals can base their choices on objective criteria. Organizations should invest in data analytics tools and training to enhance data literacy among employees.

Implementing clear decision-making processes can ensure that decisions are made systematically and transparently. Organizations can develop standardized protocols for evaluating options, gathering input, and assessing outcomes. This structured approach can help mitigate biases by ensuring that all relevant factors are considered. Keeping records of decision-making processes can enhance accountability and facilitate reflection. Documenting the rationale behind decisions, including the considerations and biases involved, allows individuals to revisit their choices and learn from past experiences. This practice can promote a culture of transparency and continuous improvement.

Creating a culture that values openness and feedback is essential for enhancing decision-making. When individuals feel safe to express their thoughts and concerns, it fosters a more robust decision-making environment.

Organizations should promote an environment where feedback is encouraged and valued. Providing opportunities for employees to share their thoughts on decisions can uncover hidden biases and alternative perspectives. Constructive feedback should be viewed as a tool for improvement rather than criticism. Implementing regular debriefs and reviews of decisions can provide opportunities for reflection and learning. After significant decisions, teams should gather to discuss what worked, what didn't, and how biases may have influenced the process. These reviews can enhance team cohesion and promote a culture of continuous learning. Mentorship programs can facilitate knowledge sharing and support the development of critical thinking skills. Pairing experienced employees with newer team members can provide valuable insights into decision-making processes. Mentors can share their experiences with biases and encourage mentees to think critically about their choices.

Fostering better decision-making through awareness and practice is a continuous journey that requires commitment and effort. By developing bias awareness, enhancing critical thinking skills, building diverse teams, implementing structured decision-making frameworks, and promoting a culture of openness and feedback, individuals and organizations can significantly improve their decision-making processes.

In an increasingly complex and fast-paced world, the ability to make informed and rational decisions is more important than ever. By addressing cognitive biases head-on and cultivating a culture that values critical thinking and continuous learning, we empower ourselves to navigate challenges with confidence and clarity. Ultimately, the goal is to create an environment where informed decision-making becomes the norm, leading to better outcomes for individuals, organizations, and society as a whole.

CHAPTER SIX

Visualizing Insights: Seeing Beyond the Numbers

As a data scientist, I often find myself immersed in raw datasets, pouring over vast amounts of numbers, looking for patterns, relationships, and anomalies. But no matter how sophisticated the analysis becomes, it's the visual representation of data that often tells the story most clearly. In the world of data science, the process of transforming raw numbers into meaningful, actionable insights is both an art and a science. At the heart of this transformation lies data visualization, a tool that has revolutionized the way we communicate complex information.

Data visualization is not just about creating aesthetically pleasing charts or graphs rather it's about enabling decision-makers to see beyond the raw numbers, to interpret the trends and patterns hidden within, and ultimately, to make better, more informed decisions. It's about helping the human brain process and understand data faster and more accurately than raw numbers alone ever could. We will learn why data visualization is a powerful tool for decision-making, how it enhances our cognitive understanding of complex datasets, and why it's indispensable in today's data-driven world.

Fundamentally, it serves as a bridge between raw data and human understanding. Let's face it: raw data can be overwhelming. A table full of numbers, even when well-organized, often doesn't communicate anything meaningful at first glance. Whether you're dealing with thousands of rows of sales data, customer behavior metrics, or website traffic logs, raw data can be difficult to interpret without the right context. In fact, research has shown that humans are much better at processing visual information than numerical data. This is because our brains are wired to identify patterns, trends, and relationships more quickly when they are presented in visual formats.

One of the most compelling reasons for visualizing data is to simplify complexity. Consider a large dataset with numerous variables, think of the kind of data that might be used to forecast sales, predict customer churn, or analyze website user behavior. When displayed in a raw tabular form, even experts can struggle to immediately understand the key trends and insights buried within the data. A scatter plot, a bar chart, or a line graph, on the other hand, can immediately highlight trends, outliers, and correlations, turning a sea of data into a clear and comprehensible story.

In fact, it's often said that a picture is worth a thousand words. And when it comes to data, this is particularly true. Consider a heatmap, for instance, which visualizes data through color gradients. In a single glance, it can reveal patterns that might take pages of raw data to articulate. It's the visual representation that unlocks the insight, not the numbers themselves. Moreover, data visualization allows us to communicate insights more effectively to others. Data is often presented to decision-makers, executives, or stakeholders who may not have a deep understanding of the underlying analytical methods or statistical models. A compelling visualization can transcend technical jargon, allowing people to understand key findings quickly and make informed decisions.

The true value of this concept lies in its ability to enhance decision-making. As decision-makers, we are often faced with a mountain of data from which we must extract meaningful insights to guide our actions. But how do we extract these insights effectively? The answer lies in the ability to see the data in ways that highlight key trends, relationships, and anomalies. Visualization enables us to sift through vast datasets and present the critical points in an easy-to-understand format, ensuring that decision-makers can act quickly and confidently. To illustrate this, let's take an example from the business world. Imagine a company that wants to understand customer churn that is why customers leave and which factors influence their decision. A raw table of customer data, with dozens of attributes such as subscription duration, customer demographics, and usage patterns, might not immediately tell the story. But by creating a simple line graph that shows customer churn rates over time or a bar chart that compares churn across different customer segments, the company's leadership can quickly see patterns and trends. Perhaps they notice that churn is particularly high among customers who have been with the company for less than six months, or that certain geographic regions exhibit significantly higher churn rates. These visual insights directly inform decisions about where to focus retention efforts or how to tailor customer service initiatives.

But the power of data visualization extends far beyond just improving decision-making as it can also prevent costly mistakes. By visualizing the data, we are more likely to identify issues before they become critical. In this way, it acts as a proactive tool, helping businesses and organizations stay ahead of potential problems by uncovering insights before they are reflected in the bottom line.

Understanding why data visualization is so powerful requires a closer look at how our brains process information. The human brain is inherently visual as it processes images and visual information far more quickly than text or numbers. In fact, studies have shown that we process visual stimuli about 60,000 times faster than text. This is one reason why visualizations are so effective: they tap into our brain's ability to process complex information rapidly.

Consider a simple example: if you see a line graph showing a company's sales growth over the past year, your brain will immediately begin processing the visual data. You'll quickly notice whether sales are trending upward or downward, and you may even start to recognize patterns that suggest seasonal fluctuations or market reactions. However, if you were given a table with the same sales data, you would need to spend far more time analyzing the numbers, comparing figures, and calculating trends in your head. The time it takes to interpret the data from a table is much longer, and there's a greater chance of missing subtle insights or making errors in judgment. This speed and efficiency in processing visual information is a result of the way our brains evolved to recognize patterns. Early humans relied on visual cues to survive, whether it was spotting a predator in the distance or recognizing the subtle differences in plant species. Over time, our brains became exceptionally good at processing visual information quickly and making split-second decisions. Today, we use this same innate skill to make sense of complex data, but with the added benefit of modern data visualization tools that allow us to amplify our cognitive abilities.

The use of color, size, and positioning in data visualization can also help direct our attention to the most important aspects of the data. These design elements play a crucial role in helping us absorb and interpret data quickly and efficiently.

One of the most powerful aspects of this mechanism is its ability to reveal the "big picture" which includes the overarching trends, correlations, and relationships that might be difficult to spot in raw data. With the right visualization, we can see not only the data itself but also how different data points are interconnected. This is particularly important when analyzing large, multidimensional datasets, where the relationships between variables are key to uncovering insights. This ability to visualize complex relationships is essential in many fields, from healthcare to finance to marketing. For example, in marketing, a well-designed visualization could show how different customer segments respond to various campaigns, enabling marketers to tailor their strategies more effectively. In finance, a visualization of stock market data over time could help investors spot trends, predict market movements, and make better investment decisions.

Beyond its cognitive benefits, data visualization is also an essential tool for communication. In many industries, data scientists and analysts are tasked with presenting findings to non-technical stakeholders, executives, clients, or team members, who may not have a deep understanding of the underlying analysis. In these cases, a well-designed visualization becomes a powerful storytelling device. It also enables real-time communication. Dashboards, for example, allow decision-makers to monitor key metrics and track progress in real time. A sales dashboard that updates automatically can give executives an immediate sense of the company's performance, allowing them to respond quickly to emerging trends or issues. This dynamic and real-time aspect of data visualization is particularly important in fast-paced industries like e-commerce, where timely decisions can make the difference between success and failure.

Data and information is growing at an exponential rate and the ability to visualize insights has become a critical skill for anyone involved in data-driven decision-making

As the amount of data in the world continues to grow at an exponential rate, understanding how to represent that data visually becomes increasingly important. Raw data, no matter how precise or extensive, only holds value when it can be understood and interpreted correctly. Let us examine the various types of data visualizations and their use cases. The choice of visualization type is crucial in ensuring that the insights drawn from the data are clear, accurate, and actionable. From basic charts to more complex visual tools, each form serves a unique purpose and is best suited to different kinds of data. By understanding which visualization method to use for which type of analysis, data scientists, analysts, and decision-makers can present data in ways that enhance understanding and guide better business decisions.

The foundational toolkits are basic visual formats such as bar charts, line graphs, and pie charts. While these visual tools might seem simple, they are foundational in presenting data clearly and effectively. Basic visualizations are ideal for displaying trends over time, comparing discrete categories, or showing distributions of data points in an easily interpretable way.

Bar charts and column charts are perhaps the most straightforward and widely recognized types of visualizations. They are used to compare the sizes or frequencies of different categories. The main distinction between the two is the orientation: bar charts are horizontal, and column charts are vertical. These charts are great for showing comparisons between categories, especially when dealing with discrete data. Additionally, stacked bar charts or grouped bar charts can be useful for comparing multiple sub-categories within each main category. For instance, a stacked bar chart could show how sales in each region are divided across different product categories, such as electronics, clothing, and home goods.

Line graphs, also known as line charts, are commonly used to depict trends or changes over time. This type of chart is particularly useful when you need to show continuous data and how it fluctuates over a period. Whether it's sales performance over the last year, temperature changes over a month, or website traffic during a week, line graphs make it easy to visualize the direction of a trend. The strength of line graphs lies in their ability to convey how a metric evolves and to highlight any fluctuations or patterns that occur across time. In addition, multiple line graphs can be overlaid on the same chart, allowing for comparative analysis.

Pie charts are another simple yet effective way to visualize data. These charts break down a whole into its constituent parts, allowing you to see proportions or percentages relative to a total. While pie charts have become somewhat controversial due to their potential for misinterpretation (especially when there are many categories or the slices are of similar size), they can still be useful when the data set is limited to just a few categories. For example, a company may use a pie chart to show the percentage of sales coming from different regions or product categories. In this case, the chart visually communicates the relative size of each category, making it clear which one dominates and which ones are smaller contributors. However, care must be taken when using pie charts to avoid overcrowding the visualization with too many categories, which can make the chart difficult to interpret.

Once we move beyond basic charts, more advanced visualizations come into play. These types of visualizations are useful for representing more nuanced data, helping to reveal deeper insights that might not be immediately obvious from simpler charts. They allow analysts to present relationships between multiple variables, distributions of data, and even correlations.

A histogram is a specialized type of bar chart used to represent the distribution of a dataset. Unlike regular bar charts, which display data for categorical variables, histograms group continuous data into intervals, or "bins." The height of each bar represents the frequency or count of data points that fall within that bin. Histograms are especially valuable when analyzing the distribution of a numerical variable, such as the distribution of ages within a population, income levels in a region, or scores on a test.

A box plot (also known as a box-and-whisker plot) provides a summary of a dataset's distribution, showing its central tendency, variability, and presence of outliers. It displays the median, quartiles, and extreme values of a dataset, offering a high-level view of the data's spread and symmetry. They are particularly useful for comparing distributions across multiple groups. Scatter plots are an excellent way to visualize the relationship between two continuous variables. Each point on the plot represents a pair of values from the two variables, allowing you to quickly see if there is any correlation between them. Scatter plots are particularly valuable in regression analysis, where you may want to investigate whether one variable can be used to predict another.

Heatmaps are a powerful tool for visualizing complex data sets in a way that is easy to interpret. By using a color gradient to represent data values, heatmaps make it possible to spot patterns, anomalies, and correlations across a matrix of data. Here, each cell in the grid is colored according to its value, with darker or more intense colors typically representing higher values. They are particularly useful in fields such as marketing, finance, and healthcare.

For more intricate or high-dimensional data, advanced visualizations offer deeper insights. These visualizations are often used when analyzing data with multiple variables or when trying to uncover non-obvious relationships between complex data points.

Network graphs are used to display relationships between entities (nodes) and the connections (edges) that link them. This visualization type is particularly useful when analyzing social networks, organizational structures, or any other data where entities interact with one another. Nodes can represent people, products, websites, or any other object, while edges represent the relationships between them. Geospatial visualizations allow data to be represented in the context of physical geography, helping to uncover patterns and trends tied to specific locations. Maps can display data points, such as customer distribution, sales by region, or even the movement of goods in a supply chain. By combining location data with other metrics, geospatial visualizations provide a unique way of interpreting data through a spatial lens.

While the types of visualizations listed here are powerful tools, the most important takeaway is that each one serves a specific purpose. The key to effective data analysis is choosing the right visualization for the task at hand. A simple pie chart might be ideal for showing the share of total sales by product category, while a scatter plot might be the better option for exploring the relationship between advertising spend and sales growth. Selecting the wrong visualization can lead to confusion or misinterpretation of the data, which undermines the decision-making process. In addition, it's important to consider the audience when selecting a method of presentation. Some stakeholders may prefer high-level summaries, while others may want a deeper dive into the details. Data scientists and analysts must tailor their visualizations to meet the needs of their audience, balancing simplicity with depth and clarity with complexity.

Data-driven decision-making is the cornerstone of modern business strategy. As businesses and organizations increasingly rely on data to guide their actions, the ability to extract actionable insights from complex datasets has become more important than ever. However, while collecting and analyzing data is crucial, the true value lies in translating these insights into concrete actions that lead to measurable outcomes.

How do we take the insights gleaned from data visualizations and turn them into actionable strategies? We will examine the process of decision-making in a data-driven environment, the importance of context, and how to align insights with business objectives. Furthermore, we will discuss the role of communication, collaboration, and continuous feedback in refining decisions and ensuring they lead to meaningful results.

The process of turning these insights into actionable decisions is neither automatic nor straightforward. It requires careful interpretation of visualized data, alignment with business objectives, and thoughtful application. A key aspect of making these decisions is understanding how to move from the analytical phase, where data is collected and visualized, to the implementation phase, where concrete actions are taken based on that data. The first step in turning insights into action is identifying the key findings from the data. Not every data point or trend will be equally important to your decision-making process. The role of data scientists and analysts is to sift through the data and uncover the most critical pieces of information that can drive business outcomes. This requires not only technical skills but also domain expertise, as the relevance of an insight can vary depending on the context. For example, a sales manager reviewing a line graph showing sales growth over the past quarter might spot a significant dip in performance during the second month. This is a critical insight that requires further investigation. The next question is, why did this dip happen? Was it due to a seasonal fluctuation, a change in marketing strategy, or some external factor like a supply chain disruption? Identifying the key insights and understanding their context is essential for moving toward action.

Once the insights have been identified, the next step is to align them with the organization's business goals. Data-driven decisions need to serve a specific purpose, whether it's increasing revenue, improving customer retention, optimizing operational efficiency, or launching a new product. The insights from the data should be framed within the context of these objectives. In some cases, aligning insights with business goals may require prioritization. Not every insight will be immediately actionable, and resources may be limited. By focusing on insights that directly impact the organization's key objectives, decision-makers can ensure that their efforts are directed toward the most impactful outcomes.

Once the insights have been aligned with business goals, the next step is to develop a strategy based on that data. A strategy is essentially a plan of action that outlines how to apply the insights to achieve the desired outcome. The strategy should detail the steps required, the resources needed, the timeline, and the specific metrics to track progress. In short, it provides a clear roadmap for turning insights into results. The strategy should also be flexible and adaptable. As data and insights evolve over time, it's important to revisit and adjust the strategy as necessary. A successful strategy should be iterative and based on feedback and continuous monitoring of results, refinements and adjustments can be made to optimize outcomes.

While data visualizations can reveal patterns, trends, and relationships, context is crucial for understanding why those insights matter. A key mistake in data-driven decision-making is relying solely on the numbers without considering the broader context in which those numbers were generated. Data is not static; it is shaped by numerous factors, including industry trends, market dynamics, and even external events. Context also plays a role in aligning insights with business goals. A company's objectives should inform how insights are interpreted and applied. For example, a sharp increase in website traffic may seem like a positive trend, but if that traffic is coming from low-value customers or bots, the action plan might need to shift toward improving customer targeting rather than simply capitalizing on increased traffic.

This concept tends to focus on quantitative insights, qualitative data and external factors which are equally important in the decision-making process. Understanding customer sentiment, industry trends, or changes in regulations can provide the necessary context for interpreting the data accurately. Customer feedback, social media discussions, competitor analysis, and macroeconomic conditions all influence the way data should be viewed. In some cases, qualitative insights can help to explain quantitative trends. For instance, a drop in customer satisfaction scores may correlate with an uptick in product returns. However, external factors such as supply chain disruptions or product recalls might be the primary cause of these trends. Understanding both the qualitative and quantitative aspects of a situation ensures that decisions are grounded in a complete view of the environment.

These decisions do not happen in a vacuum. They require collaboration and communication across various teams and departments. Analysts, data scientists, and decision-makers must work together to ensure that the insights drawn from data are effectively communicated and acted upon.

Effective communication is pivotal to translating insights into action. Data visualization tools, such as dashboards and reports, play a crucial role in presenting insights in a way that is clear and easy to understand. However, it's not just about creating visually appealing charts and graphs. The goal is to ensure that the message behind the data is clear and actionable. Communication should involve more than just presenting data. It's important to discuss the "why" behind the data and to provide context for stakeholders. This may involve highlighting assumptions, explaining the methodology, and outlining potential risks. This holistic approach fosters a deeper understanding of the data and creates a shared foundation for action.

The decision-making process is rarely a one-person task. It often requires input and collaboration from various teams such as marketing, finance, operations, and customer service, among others. Insights from data may reveal opportunities or challenges that require a collective response. For example, if an analysis reveals that customer churn is highest among users who haven't engaged with the company's app in the last 30 days, the marketing team might want to target these users with personalized re-engagement campaigns, while the product team might consider implementing new features to increase app usage.

Collaboration also ensures that decisions are well-rounded and take into account multiple perspectives. Making data-driven decisions is an iterative process. Once action is taken, it's crucial to continuously monitor the results and gather feedback to determine whether the decision was effective.

Key Performance Indicators (KPIs) are essential for measuring the success of these decisions. By tracking KPIs over time, decision-makers can assess whether the desired outcomes are being achieved and adjust strategies if necessary. A powerful method for refining these decisions is through A/B testing and experimentation. By running controlled experiments, businesses can test different approaches and measure their effectiveness.

CHAPTER SEVEN

Integrating Ethics in Data

Ethical considerations have become as critical as technical expertise. Data, as a powerful asset, holds the potential to drive significant business value, optimize decision-making, and solve complex societal problems. However, when misused or mishandled, data can also perpetuate harm, amplify inequalities, and erode trust. With great power comes great responsibility, and data professionals must be acutely aware of the ethical challenges inherent in their work.

The role of data science is becoming ever more central in various fields, from healthcare to finance, education to government, and beyond. Algorithms make decisions that affect lives, from determining who gets a loan or a job, to diagnosing medical conditions, or predicting a person's behavior. Data is no longer just a tool for analysis as it is an integral part of how modern society operates, and therefore it must be treated with the utmost care and consideration. This brings us to the heart of ethical issues in data science: how can we ensure that data is used in ways that are fair, responsible, and transparent?

One of the foundational ethical concerns is privacy specifically how personal information is collected, stored, and shared. With the growth of big data, cloud computing, and machine learning, vast amounts of personal information are being generated and processed. From the moment individuals interact with websites, use mobile apps, or engage with social media, personal data is being captured. This data often includes sensitive details like medical history, financial records, location information, or behavioral patterns. Given the potential risks involved in mishandling such sensitive data, privacy must be a primary concern.

The notion of informed consent is a key principle in privacy ethics. In the context of data collection, individuals must be made aware of what data is being collected, how it will be used, and who will have access to it. This concept is not limited to legal requirements; it's also a matter of fairness. The GDPR (General Data Protection Regulation) is one of the most well-known regulations that mandates explicit consent for data collection, requiring businesses to inform users about their data practices in clear, understandable terms. However, the complexity of modern data systems often makes obtaining informed consent challenging. For example, many users agree to lengthy privacy policies with little understanding of the implications. Some argue that these policies are intentionally opaque, leaving individuals unaware of the data they are relinquishing or how it will be used. Ethical data practices go beyond meeting legal obligations as they involve respecting the rights of individuals and ensuring that they have genuine control over their personal information.

Another critical ethical issue within privacy is the concept of data minimization. Data scientists should adhere to the principle of collecting only the data that is necessary to fulfill the intended purpose. Unnecessary or excessive data collection exposes individuals to greater risks, such as the potential for data breaches or misuse. In addition to minimizing the data collected, organizations should also prioritize data anonymization or pseudonymization. By stripping personal identifiers from data sets, the risk of privacy violations is significantly reduced. Anonymization ensures that the data cannot be traced back to an individual, while pseudonymization allows for the removal of identifiable elements while retaining certain aspects that might be useful for analysis. Ethical considerations around anonymization involve ensuring that data is protected throughout its lifecycle and that individuals' identities are safeguarded.

A second area of concern is the increasing use of surveillance technologies to monitor and track individuals. Data scientists must consider the ethical ramifications of tracking users through cookies, geolocation data, or facial recognition. The use of such technologies can blur the lines between legitimate use and intrusive surveillance. These practices raise questions about individual autonomy and freedom. Who controls this data, and how transparent are they about its use? Does surveillance infringe on people's right to privacy, or can it be justified in specific contexts (such as national security or public health)?

Bias is a pervasive and complex ethical issue in data science. Since data models and machine learning algorithms are only as good as the data they are trained on, the risk of bias is inherent. Bias in data can arise from various sources historical biases, sampling biases, or algorithmic biases all of which can lead to unfair or discriminatory outcomes. Historical bias occurs when past decisions or societal trends are reflected in the data used to train algorithms. This issue becomes more problematic when such tools are used to make decisions that affect people's lives, such as sentencing or parole decisions.

Sampling bias occurs when the data used to train models does not accurately represent the population it is intended to serve. For example, if a hiring algorithm is trained on data from predominantly male employees, it may be biased against women, assuming that male employees are more likely to succeed in the role. This issue highlights the importance of ensuring that training data is diverse and representative of all relevant groups. Algorithmic bias arises from the design of the algorithms themselves. Even if data is well-represented and free from historical biases, the way in which algorithms are structured and make decisions can still introduce bias.

Ethical data science demands that data scientists actively identify, mitigate, and correct these biases. One approach to addressing algorithmic bias is through fairness metrics which help quantify the degree of bias in a model's predictions. By evaluating the outcomes of different groups and ensuring equitable treatment, organizations can design models that are more likely to be fair and just. Furthermore, organizations should take a holistic view of fairness, recognizing that fairness can mean different things in different contexts. For instance, fairness in lending may mean providing equal access to credit regardless of race or gender, while fairness in healthcare may mean ensuring that medical treatments are accessible to all socioeconomic groups, irrespective of income or geography.

Bias in data models can also lead to discrimination, particularly against marginalized groups. It is crucial that organizations not only work to reduce bias but also assess whether their data models might reinforce existing societal inequalities. Discrimination could be as overt as rejecting qualified candidates based on race or gender or as subtle as providing unequal access to services based on zip codes or other demographic factors. As AI systems become more pervasive, particularly in areas such as hiring, criminal justice, healthcare, and finance, the risk of discrimination grows. In these domains, the stakes are higher because biases can affect individuals' livelihoods, freedoms, and access to essential services. Therefore, the ethical imperative is to design systems that actively reduce inequality and ensure fair treatment for all individuals.

Transparency and accountability are central to ethical data practices. In an era where algorithms and data-driven decisions impact almost every aspect of daily life, stakeholders including consumers, employees, and policymakers have a right to understand how decisions are made and the rationale behind them. However, many data models, particularly complex machine learning models, function as "black boxes," making it difficult for even their creators to explain how they arrive at specific conclusions.

A key ethical principle is that data systems should be explainable and interpretable. This involves ensuring that the reasoning behind data-driven decisions is accessible and understandable. In the realm of hiring, credit scoring, and criminal justice, data-driven decisions can have profound impacts on individuals' lives. If someone is denied a loan or is incarcerated based on an algorithm's prediction, they should have the ability to understand why the decision was made. Explainable AI (XAI) is a growing field that aims to make machine learning models more transparent and interpretable, providing a clearer understanding of how predictions are made and what factors influenced those predictions.

With great power comes great responsibility. Data-driven systems must be auditable meaning there should be mechanisms for reviewing and tracking how decisions are made, and who is responsible for them. This includes maintaining detailed logs of data processing, model development, and decision-making processes. Accountability ensures that there is a clear line of responsibility for outcomes, whether they are positive or negative. When data-driven decisions go wrong, such as in the case of biased models or data breaches, accountability becomes essential. Organizations must have processes in place to assess the ethical implications of their decisions, respond to complaints, and make necessary corrections. Failure to establish accountability can lead to a loss of trust, which is particularly damaging in an era of increasing reliance on data and technology.

As we move towards more autonomous systems, the need for transparency and accountability grows even more urgent. Many modern AI systems such as autonomous vehicles, financial trading algorithms, or credit scoring models make decisions without direct human intervention. In these scenarios, it becomes particularly difficult to determine who is responsible when things go wrong. If an autonomous vehicle causes an accident or an AI system makes a biased decision, how do we assign accountability?

Ethical guidelines and regulations must evolve to address these emerging challenges. While data scientists and engineers may build and design systems, ethical responsibility extends to organizations, policymakers, and society as a whole. Ethical frameworks should ensure that human oversight remains a key component of any autonomous system, allowing for intervention and accountability in cases where algorithms might cause harm.

Data ownership and informed consent are fundamental ethical issues in the realm of data science. Who owns the data, and how can individuals control what happens to their data once it is collected? This question is particularly relevant as more personal data is collected from individuals through smartphones, social media platforms, wearables, and online interactions. In many cases, individuals may unknowingly forfeit ownership of their personal data when they sign terms and conditions on digital platforms. However, individuals should retain a degree of control over their data. Ethical data practices include ensuring that data is collected transparently, that individuals can opt-out or withdraw consent at any time, and that individuals are given the opportunity to delete their data if they so choose.

Organizations must also consider the implications of using data in ways that may not align with the original intent of the consent. For example, if data collected for one purpose say, to improve customer service is later used for targeted advertising or sold to third parties, this could violate ethical principles of consent and transparency.

The ethical challenges surrounding data science are vast, complex, and multifaceted. Privacy, bias, fairness, transparency, accountability, consent, and ownership are just a few of the key issues that data professionals must consider. The evolving nature of technology means that new ethical challenges will continue to emerge, and the field of data science must be proactive in addressing them. Ethical practices in data science are not only about avoiding harm but also about ensuring that data is used to create positive, inclusive, and equitable outcomes for individuals and society as a whole.

As the role of data in shaping business decisions, public policy, and technology continues to expand, ethical considerations must be embedded throughout the entire data lifecycle. This means integrating ethical principles not only at the beginning, during the collection of information, but also throughout the stages of processing, analysis, interpretation, and application. The process of embedding ethics into data-driven systems is not a one-time effort but an ongoing, consistent commitment to ensuring that data is used responsibly, transparently, and equitably.

The data lifecycle spans a series of stages, each of which presents its own set of ethical challenges. These stages include data collection, data cleaning and preparation, data analysis and modeling, decision-making, and the application of insights. If any of these phases are approached without careful attention to ethical principles, the entire process can lead to biased conclusions, harmful practices, or the violation of privacy. We will explore how data professionals and organizations can incorporate ethics into each stage of the lifecycle, ensuring that ethical concerns are proactively addressed from start to finish.

The foundation of ethical data practices begins at the point of data acquisition. Whether an organization is gathering data from external sources (such as surveys, social media, or third-party providers) or collecting information directly from individuals (such as through websites, mobile applications, or sensors), ethical principles must guide the way data is gathered, consented to, and stored. One of the primary ethical concerns at this stage is informed consent. Individuals whose data is being collected must be fully aware of what information is being gathered, how it will be used, and who will have access to it. Informed consent is not just about asking individuals for permission; it's about ensuring they understand the potential implications of sharing their data. Ethical data practices require that organizations clearly communicate their data collection policies, not only at the point of collection but also as those policies evolve over time. For instance, online platforms often ask users to agree to lengthy privacy policies or terms of service. However, research shows that many users click through these agreements without fully understanding their contents. Ethical data practices demand transparency and clarity, ensuring that users aren't merely prompted to "agree" but are actively informed of how their data will be used. Organizations must go beyond vague or legalistic language and adopt clear, concise explanations that ensure individuals understand what they are consenting to.

A key ethical principle in the collection process is data minimization. The principle of data minimization stipulates that only the data necessary to fulfill the specific purpose should be collected. Ethical data practices emphasize that organizations must avoid the temptation to over-collect or hoard data that isn't strictly needed. This helps mitigate the risks of personal data misuse or breaches, as well as reduces the potential for unethical uses of data down the line.

Certain types of data require additional ethical safeguards. This includes sensitive information, such as health data, financial records, racial or ethnic information, and data related to sexual orientation or political affiliation. In many jurisdictions, such data is subject to stringent legal protections (e.g., the Health Insurance Portability and Accountability Act in the United States or the General Data Protection Regulation (GDPR) in Europe). But ethical practices go beyond legal compliance as they involve respecting individuals' rights to privacy and dignity, even when data may not be legally protected. Ethical data acquisition means that special care must be taken when dealing with sensitive information; including obtaining explicit consent and ensuring that this data is stored and processed with the utmost care.

Once data has been collected, it typically undergoes a process of cleaning and preparation. During this phase, the data is examined for errors, inconsistencies, and missing values. However, this process isn't just about making the data "tidy" for analysis; it also involves ensuring that the data is fair and representative, and that no biases are introduced into the dataset at this early stage. Bias can enter the data preparation phase in various ways, and these biases must be identified and addressed to avoid reinforcing unfair practices later in the data lifecycle. One of the most common forms of bias in data preparation is sampling bias, which occurs when the data collected is not representative of the broader population or situation being studied.

Another ethical concern during data preparation is how to handle missing data. Data scientists have several options for dealing with missing values, such as imputation (replacing missing data with calculated estimates) or simply excluding incomplete records. However, the way missing data is handled can introduce its own biases. Ethical practices during data cleaning include ensuring that missing data is treated in a way that minimizes bias and does not disadvantage certain groups. When possible, data scientists should explore why data is missing and make informed decisions about how to handle it in a way that reflects ethical principles of fairness and accuracy.

Maintaining data integrity during cleaning is another vital aspect as it ensures that the data remains accurate, reliable, and authentic throughout the process. Data scientists must ensure that they are not introducing errors or manipulating the data to fit a particular narrative. Integrity also involves ensuring that data is not tampered with or altered in ways that could mislead decision-makers or stakeholders.

The next stage in the data lifecycle is data analysis and modeling. During this phase, data scientists create models, run analyses, and extract insights from the data. This stage is crucial because it can influence decision-making in significant ways. Whether it's determining credit scores, identifying job candidates, diagnosing medical conditions, or targeting advertisements, the results of data analysis and modeling can have a profound impact on individuals and society. Thus, ethical considerations must be woven into the design, development, and deployment of data models. As data scientists develop models, they must be mindful of algorithmic bias, which occurs when an algorithm produces unfair or discriminatory results. Even if data is collected fairly and cleaned properly, the model itself may perpetuate bias if the algorithm is not designed to account for social, cultural, or demographic factors.

Ethical data practices in this stage also involve choosing the right features for the model and ensuring that variables are not unintentionally biased. For example, a model that predicts loan eligibility should not use variables like gender, race, or ethnicity, which may correlate with other factors but are irrelevant to a person's ability to repay a loan. Another crucial ethical consideration in modeling is explain ability. As machine learning models become more complex, particularly with the advent of deep learning and neural networks, it can become difficult to understand how a model arrived at a particular decision. Ethical data practices emphasize the importance of explainable AI (XAI) which is the idea that machine learning systems should be interpretable by humans and transparent in how they make decisions.

Ethical modeling also requires ongoing monitoring and evaluation. Models should not be "set and forgotten." Over time, data shifts and societal changes can cause models to become outdated or less effective. Regular audits, adjustments, and recalibrations are necessary to ensure that models continue to perform ethically and without unintended biases. These considerations should be an ongoing process rather than a one-time check.

The final stage of the data lifecycle involves applying the insights derived from analysis and models. In this phase, the focus shifts from raw numbers to real-world consequences. The ethical use of data at this stage is critical, as decisions based on data-driven insights can have far-reaching implications for individuals and society.

One of the most important ethical concerns in data application is ensuring fairness in decision-making. Whether the data is being used to determine who receives a job offer, who gets a loan, or who is approved for healthcare coverage, the decisions that follow must be fair and just. Data-driven decision-making should not disproportionately affect certain groups, especially those who are already marginalized or vulnerable. Organizations should implement safeguards to ensure that decisions made with data are consistent with ethical principles of fairness. This may involve using fairness audits, collecting feedback from stakeholders, and validating decisions against diverse data sets to ensure that the outcomes are not skewed by bias.

Finally, transparency and accountability must be maintained when applying these insights. Stakeholders must be able to understand how decisions are made and who is responsible for those decisions. When something goes wrong whether it's a discriminatory decision, an error in data processing, or a privacy violation, accountability ensures that there is a process in place to address the issue, correct mistakes, and make reparations where necessary.

Creating an Ethical Data Culture: Leadership and Organizational Responsibility

The rapid growth of data-driven technologies has made it increasingly clear that ethical considerations must be at the forefront of decision-making. Whether it's artificial intelligence (AI), machine learning, big data analytics, or other emerging technologies, the way data is handled has significant implications for individuals, society, and the organizations that deploy these tools. However, ethical issues in data science and analytics cannot be fully addressed by merely establishing guidelines or regulations. In order to truly effect meaningful change, it is imperative for an organization to create an ethical data culture which is one that integrates ethics into every facet of its data practices, from the data collection phase to the use of data in decision-making.

An ethical data culture is one where responsible use of data is prioritized, and where ethical considerations are embedded in organizational processes, leadership decisions, and day-to-day operations. It goes beyond compliance with privacy laws or the adoption of ethical frameworks, it's a culture shift that involves a collective commitment to acting with integrity and accountability when working with data. In this section, we will explore how organizations can establish a culture of ethical data practices. We will examine the role of leadership in fostering this culture, the importance of training and employee engagement, and the structural changes needed to integrate ethics into data workflows. By the end of this section, we will have a roadmap for how organizations can create and sustain an ethical data culture that is not just theoretical, but practical and actionable.

Creating this culture begins with leadership. Leaders whether in executive roles, data science teams, or across other departments are responsible for establishing the vision, values, and principles that guide how data is handled within an organization. This leadership must be vocal, proactive, and committed to ethics as a core component of the organization's identity.

At the very top of an organization, the leadership must set the tone for ethical data use. It's the responsibility of executives and board members to define the organization's stance on data ethics, ensuring that it aligns with broader organizational goals and societal responsibilities. If ethical considerations are not prioritized at the highest levels of an organization, it's unlikely that they will be fully embraced by staff members and employees lower down the chain. Creating an ethical data culture requires clear ethical guidelines and values statements that reflect a commitment to responsible practices. This involves defining what is considered ethical behavior in the context of data collection, analysis, use, and sharing. Key aspects of these guidelines include:

- Transparency: Ensuring that all stakeholders, both internal and external, are informed about the organization's data practices and policies.
- Accountability: Assigning responsibility for the ethical use of data at all levels, ensuring that individuals and teams are held accountable for their actions.
- Fairness: Emphasizing the importance of fairness in data-driven decision-making, ensuring that data practices do not disproportionately harm or benefit specific groups.

- Privacy and Security: A commitment to protecting the privacy and security of individuals' data, ensuring that it is stored and used in compliance with relevant laws and best practices.

Having a leadership-driven commitment to these values creates a foundation upon which ethical practices can be built across the organization. Leaders must also be willing to communicate these principles clearly and consistently to employees and stakeholders, embedding them in the organizational culture. In addition to setting the tone, leadership must also build systems of accountability that reinforce ethical data practices. This means establishing roles or departments dedicated to overseeing ethical issues related to data. This could include the creation of data ethics committees or advisory boards, consisting of representatives from various departments (e.g., legal, data science, HR, compliance) that meet regularly to review data practices and discuss ethical concerns.

Data governance frameworks that include ethical considerations as a core element of managing and overseeing data use should also be incorporated. This could involve setting up formal oversight mechanisms to ensure that data is being handled in an ethical and responsible manner across departments. For example, an organization may create a chief data officer (CDO) role whose responsibilities include overseeing the ethical use of data and ensuring that company policies align with ethical standards. Similarly, regular audits and reviews of data practices can be institutionalized to identify potential ethical issues before they become problematic.

Leaders must not only talk about the importance of ethical data practices rather they must lead by example. This means that when leadership makes decisions about data or technology, ethical considerations should be explicitly factored into the decision-making process. This includes using data ethically in internal decision-making (such as hiring, promotions, and performance evaluations) as well as in business operations. When leadership demonstrates a commitment to ethics in their data use, it sets a powerful example for employees at all levels. If leadership prioritizes ethical considerations in its decisions, employees will be more likely to follow suit. Conversely, if leaders ignore ethical concerns in favor of short-term gains, it sends a message that data can be used irresponsibly, leading to potential harm.

An ethical data culture isn't something that can be created by leaders alone; it requires widespread buy-in from employees at all levels. Employees whether they are directly involved in data analysis or not must be aware of ethical principles related to data, and how they relate to the work they do.

One of the most effective ways to promote this awareness across the organization is through training and education programs. These programs should be designed to ensure that every employee whether a data scientist, a marketing professional, or a product manager understands the ethical issues at play in their use of data. Training should cover topics such as data privacy and the importance of protecting sensitive information, bias and fairness in data collection, analysis, and modeling, and how to recognize and address potential issues, transparency and explain ability in machine learning and AI, and why it's important to ensure that data-driven decisions are interpretable and accountability and responsibility for ethical data use, and how to report unethical practices or concerns.

These training programs should be ongoing and updated regularly to reflect new developments in both technology and data ethics. In addition, organizations may consider creating a formal code of ethics or ethical guidelines document that all employees must review and acknowledge, ensuring that they are familiar with the organization's stance on data ethics.

An important part of building this culture is encouraging employee participation in shaping the ethical direction of the organization. This could involve creating forums where employees can raise concerns or suggest improvements to data practices. A whistleblower policy can also empower employees to report unethical behavior without fear of retaliation. By giving employees a voice in decision-making, organizations can ensure that ethical issues are more likely to be identified early and addressed in a timely manner. Empowering employees also means creating an environment where they feel supported and equipped to make ethical decisions. If employees face ethical dilemmas related to data, they should have access to resources, such as ethics advisory teams or legal counsel, to help them navigate these challenges. By providing tools and frameworks to guide ethical decision-making, organizations ensure that employees feel confident in acting in line with the organization's values.

They can also develop the appropriate structural processes to ensure that data practices align with ethical standards. These processes must be embedded throughout the organization and be a core part of the workflow in departments that handle data. A robust data governance framework is essential for ensuring that ethical considerations are integrated into day-to-day data practices. This refers to the policies, procedures, and standards that govern the collection, management, and use of data within an organization. It involves establishing clear roles and responsibilities for managing data, ensuring its quality, protecting it from misuse, and ensuring that its use complies with relevant laws and ethical standards.

An effective data governance framework includes clear definitions of roles and responsibilities regarding data management, including oversight of ethical concerns. It also covers protocols for auditing and monitoring data use to ensure compliance with ethical standards and regular reviews and assessments of data practices to ensure they are aligned with evolving laws, regulations, and best practices. Additionally, organizations should ensure that their data governance framework accounts for issues like data lineage, data retention, and data access controls, all of which can have ethical implications.

Organizations that deploy AI systems and machine learning models must ensure that their algorithms are built and monitored with ethics in mind. This requires the implementation of algorithmic governance practices, which ensure that algorithms are developed transparently, tested for fairness, and regularly audited to prevent biases from being perpetuated. Algorithmic governance may involve setting up specific ethics review boards for AI systems, where diverse teams including ethicists, technologists, and domain experts review the system's design, data inputs, and potential outcomes to identify any ethical risks. These boards can help ensure that AI and machine learning systems align with the organization's ethical standards before being deployed at scale.

Finally, organizations should measure and monitor their ethical performance when it comes to data practices. This includes establishing key performance indicators (KPIs) for ethical data use. For example, organizations could measure the rate of bias or discrimination in their decision-making processes. They could also measure employee and customer satisfaction with the transparency and fairness of data practices and compliance with privacy and security standards. Metrics help organizations track their progress in fostering an ethical data culture and ensure accountability for maintaining ethical standards over time.

Creating an ethical data culture is not a one-off project, but a continual and evolving commitment that involves leadership, education, and institutionalized processes. Leaders play a central role in setting the tone and making ethical data use a priority. Employees must be empowered with the knowledge and tools to make ethical decisions and processes must be in place to ensure that data is handled responsibly at every stage of its lifecycle. Through these combined efforts, organizations can foster a culture where data ethics are not just a checkbox or compliance requirement, but a core value that drives how the organization operates, makes decisions, and serves its customers and communities. By embedding ethics into every aspect of the data process, organizations not only reduce the risk of harm and legal liability but also build trust with their stakeholders. Ethical data use leads to more equitable outcomes, more transparent decision-making, and a better future for all.

CHAPTER EIGHT

Everyday Analytics: Making Data Work for You

I n the age of information, data is everywhere. From the apps on our smartphones to the choices we make in our daily routines, we are constantly generating and interacting with data. Yet, despite its ubiquity, many of us don't fully harness the power of this data to improve our everyday lives. In this chapter, we will explore how everyday people which are individuals like you and me can use data to enhance personal decision-making, improve productivity, boost health and wellness, and even make better financial choices. The power of data isn't just reserved for large corporations or tech-savvy professionals; it can be a valuable tool for everyone.

This chapter will break down the practical steps for integrating data analytics into our personal lives. By exploring how to collect, interpret, and apply data, we'll see how everyday analytics can empower individuals to make smarter, more informed decisions. We'll focus on three key areas where individuals can harness the power of data namely using data for personal decision-making, optimizing health and wellness with data and improving financial well-being through data amongst others.

Data is not just for businesses, but for anyone looking to make better, more informed decisions. From figuring out the best time to purchase something to understanding which daily habits improve or hinder our well-being, data can provide powerful insights into all aspects of life. With the tools and technologies available today, we have the opportunity to track and analyze our actions, preferences, and outcomes allowing us to make smarter decisions based on real evidence rather than guesswork or intuition alone. One of the simplest ways to begin using data in daily life is by tracking personal preferences and behaviors. Have you ever wondered what time of day you're most productive? Or how much sleep you really need to feel rested? Using basic tools such as note-taking apps, habit trackers, or even spreadsheets, we can record and visualize patterns in our behavior over time.

For example, tracking sleep patterns through an app like Sleep Cycle or a fitness tracker such as Fitbit or Apple Watch can provide insights into how your sleep quality correlates with your mood, productivity, or energy levels. By gathering data on how much sleep you're getting, how often you wake up during the night, and how rested you feel in the morning, you can make more informed decisions about adjusting your bedtime routine or lifestyle habits to improve your sleep. Similarly, you can track your time management throughout the day. By logging how much time you spend on various tasks such as work, social media, exercise, chores you may notice trends that can be optimized. For example, a person might find that they are more productive in the morning after exercise, and this insight might encourage them to schedule important tasks in the early hours, or dedicate the afternoon for creative work. Tracking this data helps eliminate trial and error and moves us closer to making better decisions that align with our goals.

Another powerful way individuals can use data in their personal lives is through more informed purchasing decisions. With the rise of comparison websites, online reviews, and price tracking tools, we can now make smarter choices about what we buy, when we buy it, and how much we're paying for it. Beyond just tracking prices, using data from customer reviews can also guide decision-making. By synthesizing user reviews, we can get a more accurate understanding of a product or service's true value and quality, rather than relying on the company's marketing alone.

In addition to tracking behaviors, individuals can collect data on their time usage to optimize productivity. A classic example of this is using the Pomodoro technique, a time-management strategy that encourages working in short bursts followed by short breaks. If you were to track the number of sessions you complete in a day, how long your breaks are, and your overall productivity levels, you could identify the times of day when you're most productive, the activities that cause distractions, and when breaks are necessary for sustained focus. With this information, you can make adjustments, set goals, and work towards greater efficiency. The key is to look at the data, identify trends, and make decisions based on real, not perceived, productivity.

One of the most significant areas where data can have a direct impact on our lives is in health and wellness. Over the past decade, the health industry has witnessed a surge in wearable technologies, fitness apps, and health-monitoring devices. These tools allow individuals to gather data on various aspects of their health, from daily activity levels to heart rate, sleep patterns, and even stress levels. By consistently tracking your metrics, individuals can identify trends and patterns in their physical health that might not be immediately obvious. For instance, you may notice that you feel more energetic and sleep better on days when you hit a specific step count or workout intensity. Or, you might realize that your heart rate spikes after consuming certain foods, helping you adjust your diet to reduce inflammation or fatigue.

By using this information to create more personalized health plans, individuals can tailor their fitness routines to their needs, rather than following generic advice. If an individual's goal is to lose weight, data from a fitness tracker can help them understand how different exercises impact their calorie burn. Alternatively, for someone looking to improve endurance, tracking the intensity of their workouts can allow for adjustments that help progressively improve fitness over time.

Another key area where data can help improve wellness is in tracking food intake. Some apps like allow users to log their meals and track caloric intake, macronutrients (carbs, fats, proteins), micronutrients (vitamins and minerals), and even water consumption. This data can help individuals make healthier food choices, prevent overconsumption, and understand how different foods affect their energy levels or mood. Over time, individuals may observe how their diet correlates with their health goals. Keeping a food diary or using food-tracking apps can help individuals avoid emotional or mindless eating, especially when paired with insights about the impact of their diet on their physical performance and mental state.

Data-driven wellness isn't limited to physical health; mental health is an equally important area where personal data can make a difference. Using feedback analyzed from the information gathered, people can build a mental health routine that works best for their needs, whether it's exercising regularly, meditating, or taking more breaks throughout the day to manage stress. By consistently collecting data on mental well-being, individuals can make more proactive decisions in managing their emotions, leading to better overall mental health.

Data can be incredibly useful when it comes to managing personal finances. By using the tools available to track spending, savings, and investment patterns, individuals can take control of their financial situation, set clear goals, and make informed decisions to ensure long-term financial health. Individuals can track their spending habits, categorize expenses, and set budgets based on real-time data using apps that provide detailed visualizations of spending patterns, showing how much money is going toward essentials (housing, utilities, groceries) and how much is being spent on discretionary items (entertainment, dining out, etc.). By analyzing this data, individuals can identify unnecessary or excessive spending and adjust their habits accordingly.

For individuals involved in investing, using data is critical for making informed choices. Through consistent tracking, people can monitor whether their investment strategy is working or if they need to make adjustments. By gathering data on how various stocks, bonds, or other assets have performed, individuals can make more informed decisions, shifting their portfolio to better align with market trends and personal financial goals. Additionally, data can help investors manage risks by providing insights into market fluctuations or identifying diversification opportunities to reduce the likelihood of significant losses.

While these metrics might seem like a tool primarily for productivity, health, or financial management, it can also be used to improve personal relationships. Whether you're looking to strengthen communication with a partner, improve family dynamics, or maintain long-distance friendships, data can help you better understand emotional patterns, identify recurring issues, and optimize the quality of your interactions. By bringing a data-driven mindset to your personal life, you can make more informed, intentional decisions that foster stronger, more fulfilling relationships.

Many people unknowingly fall into communication traps in their relationships. They might not recognize when they are spending too little quality time with a loved one or when a certain topic consistently leads to conflict. Through data collection, we can uncover patterns that can inform better communication and relational strategies. For example, using a relationship journal app, you can track your interactions, moods, and feelings about conversations or conflicts. You could log when you feel disconnected, what issues arise repeatedly, or what topics seem to lead to more harmonious exchanges. This data can highlight areas of improvement, like ensuring you and your partner dedicate time to discussions about your relationship, addressing issues promptly rather than letting them fester, or noticing when certain external factors (such as stress from work) influence the dynamics.

In the context of family and household management, data can also play a role in organizing tasks and improving cooperation. Using a shared calendar, families can track appointments, school events, and family obligations. This ensures that no one is left out or overburdened with responsibilities. Data can also be used to track household chores, who has completed which tasks, which tasks are overdue, and when to rotate responsibilities. Using these simple tools, families can run more smoothly, reducing stress and increasing cooperation.

In more complex or challenging relationships such as with colleagues, extended family members, or even friends, data can also assist in building emotional intelligence (EQ) and improving conflict resolution. By tracking your own emotional responses and patterns, you can gain insight into what triggers emotional reactions and how best to handle these situations. Tools such as Relish or Lasting offer structured activities for couples to resolve conflicts or enhance communication skills. These platforms use data on your interactions to tailor advice, making it easier to develop strategies for dealing with disagreements and building trust.

Social interactions also benefit from data-driven approaches. For example, keeping track of social media usage and the emotional impact of online interactions can help individuals create healthier boundaries and more meaningful connections. Recognizing that certain platforms might leave you feeling drained or overwhelmed allows you to make intentional choices about how you engage with online communities.

Another area where individuals can make data work for them is through personal growth and learning. Whether you're pursuing new skills, striving to become more knowledgeable in a particular field, or working on personal development, collecting and analyzing data about your learning progress can be immensely valuable. Data-driven learning strategies can help you stay focused, identify strengths and weaknesses, and optimize your personal development.

The first step in using data for personal growth is setting clear, measurable learning goals. Whether you're learning a new language, mastering a musical instrument, or trying to develop a new professional skill, creating specific targets will help you measure your progress effectively. If you're learning a new language, you might set goals such as mastering 50 new words per week or practicing conversation for 30 minutes a day. Language-learning apps like Duolingo track your progress and give you data-driven feedback on areas where you need improvement. These apps often show you statistics about your daily streaks, accuracy, and completion rates, allowing you to visualize how much progress you've made. Similarly, apps like Coursera, Udemy, or LinkedIn Learning offer data insights into your learning journey. These platforms track your course completion rates, test scores, and time spent on various lessons. Over time, you can analyze this data to determine which types of learning methods or materials are most effective for you and which areas require more focus.

Through data analysis, you can also gain insights into your personal strengths and weaknesses. Learning analytics tools track your engagement, performance, and completion times, giving you an overall view of your capabilities. By analyzing this data, you can identify patterns that show you what skills you excel at and where you may need extra practice.

It can also help individuals become more efficient in their learning process. Time tracking tools allow individuals to measure how much time they are dedicating to specific tasks or learning goals. By reviewing the data from these tools, you can assess whether you are spending too much time on certain activities or neglecting areas that require more focus. The information you collect about your learning progress can also be used to set personal milestones and rewards. Research has shown that the psychology of reward is crucial to maintaining motivation. By breaking down long-term learning goals into smaller, trackable milestones, you can maintain your enthusiasm and celebrate achievements along the way.

Finally, data can facilitate continuous learning by creating feedback loops. By tracking and analyzing your progress over time, you are constantly collecting data that can inform your next steps. Conversely, if the data shows that you are not progressing as fast as you had hoped, you can evaluate your learning methods, adjust your study techniques, or seek additional resources. This iterative process allows for ongoing refinement of your learning strategies, ensuring that you continue improving efficiently and effectively.

The tools and methods for making data work in our daily lives are now more accessible than ever, offering individuals a unique opportunity to transform how they live, work, and relate to others. By embracing everyday analytics, people can harness data to lead more intentional, informed, and fulfilling lives. Whether it is managing finances, improving relationships, or achieving personal growth, data offers the potential to unlock a new level of self-awareness and positive change.

CHAPTER NINE

Collaborative Intelligence:
Harnessing Collective Insights

Collaborative intelligence is a powerful tool that leverages the collective wisdom, experiences, and knowledge of individuals to solve complex problems, make better decisions, and innovate. Unlike individual intelligence, which draws from one person's perspective and experience, collaborative intelligence combines the insights of many people, often with diverse skills, backgrounds, and areas of expertise. By tapping into this collective knowledge, individuals and organizations can arrive at solutions that no single person might have thought of alone.

This intelligence refers to the idea that groups of individuals whether teams, communities, or even large-scale crowds can work together to process, analyze, and generate insights from data in ways that are more effective than working in isolation. It's the synergy of diverse minds coming together to solve problems, create solutions, and make informed decisions. This collaboration isn't limited to face-to-face interactions or small teams but can extend to the power of global networks, digital platforms, and crowdsourcing.

The collaborative process can be seen in various forms, such as crowdsourcing which is when a large group of people are invited to contribute ideas, feedback, or solutions to a particular challenge or question. Open-source collaboration refers to where individuals with different skill sets contribute to the development of projects, software, or solutions that are freely available to others. Team-based problem-solving is where a team of experts from various fields works together to analyze data and generate insights that would be difficult for one person to produce alone. In all of these scenarios, the key is to combine individual knowledge and insights into a collective intelligence that enhances creativity, decision-making, and innovation.

The effectiveness of collaborative intelligence is rooted in several psychological and practical principles that underpin human interaction and decision-making such as

- **Diversity of Thought:** Groups of people with different backgrounds, expertise, and perspectives can offer more varied solutions to a problem. The diversity of thought challenges assumptions and introduces new angles that might not be considered in homogenous groups. As the saying goes, "Two heads are better than one," but when those heads come from different disciplines, cultural backgrounds, or expertise, the solutions can be even more innovative.

- **Synergy:** The concept of synergy is where the combined efforts of a group produce a result greater than the sum of individual efforts and drives collaborative intelligence. When individuals contribute their ideas, data, and knowledge, the group can iterate, refine, and build on each other's contributions, resulting in more sophisticated, comprehensive solutions.

- **Distributed Intelligence:** Collaborative intelligence thrives in environments where knowledge is distributed, and individuals bring their specific expertise to the table. Instead of having one person responsible for all aspects of a problem, each person or team member can focus on their area of expertise. This distributed approach allows for deeper analysis, faster innovation, and more well-rounded solutions.

- **Access to Data and Technology:** Digital tools, cloud-based platforms, and collaborative technologies (like Google Workspace, Slack, Trello, Miro, and other collaboration software) make it easier for teams to work together in real-time, share insights, and collectively make sense of large amounts of data. Technology has made it possible for people in different geographical locations and time zones to come together and contribute their insights. This has expanded the reach and power of collaborative intelligence globally.

- **Cross-Pollination of Ideas:** When individuals with different skill sets and experiences collaborate, there is an opportunity for the cross-pollination of ideas. These cross-disciplinary collaborations often result in creative solutions and innovative outcomes. For example, a data scientist working with a psychologist and a marketer can generate unique insights into consumer behavior by integrating different perspectives into their analysis.

Collaborative intelligence can be applied to a variety of complex, real-world problems across industries and fields. The following examples highlight how collective insights can solve challenges that require creativity, diverse thinking, and access to data.

It plays a significant role in advancing healthcare. By pooling data from hospitals, research institutions, and public health organizations, researchers can identify trends, discover new treatments, and improve patient care. During the COVID-19 pandemic, for example, global health agencies collaborated on research data to understand the virus, develop vaccines, and distribute resources more effectively. The speed and success of vaccine development were, in part, due to the power of collaborative intelligence in medical and scientific communities.

Solving global environmental issues, such as climate change or biodiversity loss, requires the collaborative effort of governments, businesses, scientists, and citizens. Data-sharing platforms like Global Forest Watch, which aggregates satellite data and crowd-sourced insights to monitor deforestation, show how data-driven collaboration can drive positive environmental change. By pooling resources, knowledge, and data, global initiatives like the Paris Agreement on climate change can leverage collaborative intelligence to address complex sustainability challenges. Companies and organizations often use crowdsourcing platforms to pose challenges to the public and tap into the collective intelligence of people around the world. This kind of innovation, driven by open collaboration, allows organizations to solve difficult problems that they may not have been able to solve internally.

Collaborative intelligence can also be used in public policy development. Platforms that allow citizens to contribute their ideas and feedback can help governments make more informed, democratic decisions. These platforms allow for open dialogue between citizens and policymakers, where diverse opinions are integrated to create more effective and inclusive policies. Collaborative intelligence can also be seen in movements like Open Government, where data and government operations are made more transparent to foster public engagement and decision-making.

In product development, it allows businesses to create products that more closely align with customer needs. Through the aggregation of customer feedback, reviews, and product testing data, companies can refine their offerings and create more successful innovations.

While the power of collaborative intelligence is clear, leveraging it effectively requires the right frameworks, tools, and strategies. Simply gathering people together is not enough to unlock the full potential of collective insights. To create a system where collaboration leads to meaningful outcomes, certain principles and practices need to be in place.

The first step in building effective collaborative intelligence is ensuring diversity in the participants. This diversity can be in terms of skills, expertise, experience, culture, and perspectives. By bringing together a broad range of individuals, you increase the likelihood that the group will come up with innovative and well-rounded solutions. A team of specialists might approach a problem from a limited angle, whereas a diverse team can generate multiple solutions that address various aspects of the issue.

Collaboration thrives when participants are aligned on a common goal. In a collaborative intelligence framework, communication must be transparent, open, and clear. All participants should understand the purpose of the collaboration, the desired outcomes, and the roles they play in achieving those outcomes. Without this alignment, collective intelligence can become fragmented, and the effort may lack direction. Although collaboration is often seen as an informal, organic process, there is value in setting up structured processes that help guide it. This could include establishing regular check-ins, defining specific deliverables or milestones, and creating processes for decision-making. Structured frameworks can also help track progress, measure outcomes, and adjust strategies as needed.

Collaborative technologies are the backbone of modern-day collaboration. Platforms like Slack, Microsoft Teams, Zoom, and Trello provide the infrastructure for seamless communication, file sharing, task management, and efficient collaboration. These tools allow for asynchronous collaboration, enabling teams to work across time zones, and they create an archive of discussions, which can be useful for future reference. It also requires data to be shared freely and transparently within the team. This could mean sharing research, feedback, metrics, and insights in a centralized, accessible way.

Beyond the tools and structures, it is essential to foster the right workplace culture. This involves encouraging open dialogue, mutual respect, and the belief that everyone's input is valuable. A culture of collaboration can be supported by leaders who model collaborative behaviors, reward team efforts, and create an environment where it's safe to experiment and fail. One of the key elements of a successful collaborative culture is building trust. Trust is crucial for sharing ideas openly, challenging assumptions, and innovating together. Trust can be built through transparent communication, inclusive decision-making, and acknowledgment of each team member's contribution.

As with any problem-solving or creative process, collaboration is most effective when it is iterative. Teams should gather feedback regularly and use that feedback to refine their approaches. This process of continuous improvement ensures that collaborative efforts evolve and lead to better outcomes over time.

Technology has also fostered the creation of virtual communities and knowledge-sharing networks that enhance collaborative intelligence. Platforms like Reddit, Stack Overflow, Quora, and GitHub have built spaces where experts and everyday users can share insights, ask questions, and help solve problems collectively. These platforms have become the backbone of innovation, enabling individuals to contribute their specialized knowledge to projects, conversations, and challenges that require input from diverse areas of expertise.

Professional networking sites like LinkedIn and niche industry-specific forums are becoming increasingly important in helping people find collaborative opportunities. These platforms enable individuals to build their personal or professional brands, connect with like-minded individuals or teams, and leverage advice and feedback to further their careers or solve work-related problems.

One of the most powerful applications of technology in collaborative intelligence is the ability to work in real-time. Tools such as Google Docs, Figma, Miro, and Notion allow multiple contributors to edit, brainstorm, and share information instantaneously, making the process of group collaboration more dynamic and efficient than ever before. This has profound implications for industries such as product design, where remote teams of designers, engineers, and marketers can come together to co-create prototypes or solutions in record time. Similarly, in business strategy or policy development, teams can collaboratively analyze data, test assumptions, and iterate solutions based on feedback from stakeholders, customers, or the public.

While the technological tools facilitating collaborative intelligence are transformative, they also introduce their own set of ethical challenges and technical hurdles. For instance, issues related to privacy and data security are exacerbated in collaborative settings where sensitive information is shared among a wide network of contributors. Data governance, intellectual property rights, and the potential for misuse of collaborative efforts are important factors to consider when developing platforms and systems for collective collaboration. Digital literacy is also a critical challenge. Even though technology has democratized collaboration, not everyone has equal access to it, nor do they all possess the skills to leverage digital tools effectively. This digital divide can limit the inclusivity of collaborative intelligence systems, making it crucial to create technologies that are accessible and user-friendly for a broad demographic.

Looking ahead, emerging technologies such as artificial intelligence, machine learning, virtual reality (VR), and augmented reality (AR) are poised to further enhance collaborative intelligence. These technologies have the potential to create even more immersive and intuitive collaborative environments, bridging the gap between physical and digital spaces.

As AI continues to advance, we can expect augmented collaboration, where machine learning models assist human teams by analyzing data faster, spotting hidden patterns, and suggesting optimized solutions. This technology may help to reduce the cognitive load on human participants, making collaboration more efficient, effective, and creative. AI-driven tools like chatbots or virtual assistants can facilitate the smooth flow of information, automate repetitive tasks, and provide real-time insights to inform decision-making processes.

However, as we advance into the future, it will be important to maintain an ethical stance in the development of these technologies. We must ensure that the benefits of collaborative intelligence continue to be shared equitably and that these technologies are used to enhance, rather than replace, human creativity and collaboration. Further development of AI ethics, responsible data practices, and inclusive design will be necessary to ensure that technology continues to empower individuals and groups to collaborate for the common good.

CHAPTER TEN

The Future of Decision-Making: Embracing Data-Driven Mindsets

Decision-making is the foundation of human behavior, whether at an individual or organizational level. Historically, decision-making was largely based on intuition, experience, and subjective judgment, a process that involved internal heuristics and reliance on personal or group expertise. These decisions, though often effective, were shaped by a myriad of factors that were difficult to measure and quantify. As we move into the age of information and advanced analytics, however, the landscape of decision-making has dramatically shifted. Today, data and technology play pivotal roles in shaping how decisions are made, leading to a more scientific, objective, and predictive approach.

Before the rise of data analytics and digital tools, decisions were typically made by individuals or groups who relied heavily on their gut feelings, past experiences, and expert judgment. In the business world, decisions were often based on market trends observed through personal interactions, limited information, or informal data sources. Leaders relied on their instincts, feedback from a small circle of trusted advisors, and their personal experiences to guide organizational direction, product development, or even human resource management.

For centuries, this form of decision-making which we might call the "traditional" model served society well. After all, this process was shaped by knowledge accumulated over time, supported by historical precedent, and tempered by wisdom passed down through generations. Leaders and organizations succeeded in environments where information was often sparse, systems were relatively simple, and competition was localized. Decisions made through intuition and experiences were deemed effective because the available information was limited, and the complexity of challenges was not as overwhelming.

However, as businesses grew larger and the globalization of markets took hold, the limitations of relying solely on intuition and experience became apparent. The complexity of managing expansive operations, global supply chains, and increasingly diverse markets required more precision and more structured decision-making. Traditional methods based on gut feelings and informal judgments were often inadequate in the face of new challenges. This shift marked the beginning of the transition from instinctive decision-making to more structured, data-based approaches.

The turning point in decision-making came with the advent of computing and the exponential growth of data in the latter half of the 20th century. The rise of information technology revolutionized how businesses operated and interacted with their customers. In the early 1990s, data management systems like Enterprise Resource Planning (ERP) software started to become mainstream. These systems allowed businesses to collect and store vast amounts of transactional data from customer purchases to inventory levels. The sheer volume of information generated by businesses and consumers paved the way for more sophisticated decision-making models based on empirical evidence rather than just intuition.

The integration of customer relationship management (CRM) systems, for example, enabled companies to analyze purchasing patterns, demographics, and buying behaviors with much greater precision. Rather than relying on anecdotal feedback or intuition about what customers wanted, businesses could now track and analyze consumer preferences properly. With the introduction of database management systems and analytics platforms, information became an asset and a powerful tool for informing decision-making across virtually every business function.

By the early 2000s, business intelligence (BI) tools, powered by more sophisticated databases and analytics engines, began to surface. Companies could now not only collect data but also process it to uncover patterns, insights, and trends. The ability to visualize data and translate complex datasets into actionable information marked a significant departure from the subjective, experience-based decisions of the past. In parallel with the rise of BI, data scientists and analysts began to emerge as specialized roles within organizations. These professionals had the expertise to analyze large datasets, apply statistical methods, and use predictive analytics tools to make more accurate forecasts. By providing organizations with quantitative evidence, these experts could guide decision-making, helping executives move away from intuition-driven choices to ones supported by rigorous data analysis.

Today, decision-making in both businesses and government is dominated by data-driven models. Whether it's a small startup or a multinational corporation, companies are increasingly relying on data analytics, machine learning, and artificial intelligence (AI) to make smarter, faster decisions. The rise of big data has allowed decision-makers to access vast amounts of information from diverse sources, including transactional records, social media activity, IoT (Internet of Things) devices, and even sensors embedded in products or environments.

Modern decision-making is no longer limited to historical data alone. Predictive analytics, which uses historical data to forecast future outcomes, plays a crucial role in decision-making today. Companies can predict consumer behavior, market shifts, supply chain disruptions, and financial risks using sophisticated algorithms and data models. Predictive analytics, powered by machine learning and deep learning techniques, is becoming increasingly accurate, allowing organizations to make decisions with a degree of certainty that was previously unimaginable.

At the organizational level, this decision-making is not confined to the C-suite or top management. With the proliferation of self-service analytics tools, employees at all levels now have access to relevant data, allowing them to make informed decisions without waiting for instructions from higher-ups. Tableau, Power BI, and other visualization tools enable teams to interact directly with data, uncover insights, and make decisions autonomously.

The shift towards data-driven decision-making offers several compelling benefits. First and foremost, it enables organizations to make informed decisions based on objective evidence, which significantly reduces the risks associated with gut-feelings or flawed assumptions. By using data as the foundation for decision-making, organizations can minimize biases, identify hidden patterns, and uncover new opportunities that would otherwise be missed. Second, data-driven approaches allow for greater precision. Predictive analytics, for example, can forecast outcomes based on historical trends, enabling decision-makers to anticipate problems and opportunities before they arise. This level of foresight can give organizations a competitive edge, allowing them to stay ahead of market shifts, customer demands, or operational inefficiencies.

Another advantage is its ability to optimize resource allocation. By analyzing data on sales, operations, and customer preferences, organizations can identify areas where resources such as personnel, capital, or inventory are being underutilized. This allows businesses to redirect their resources more efficiently, increasing profitability and reducing waste. It can significantly improve the speed of decision-making. In industries where time is critical, such as logistics, e-commerce, or customer service, the ability to quickly process and interpret data enables organizations to respond to changing conditions with agility. Whether it's adjusting a marketing campaign based on customer feedback or rerouting a shipment to avoid delays, data empowers decision-makers to act quickly and confidently.

Despite its many advantages, embracing a data-driven mindset comes with its own set of challenges. One of the primary hurdles is the quality of data. If the data being used is inaccurate, outdated, or incomplete, the decisions based on that data are likely to be flawed. Ensuring the integrity and reliability of data is essential to the success of any decision-making process.

Data overload is also a common issue. The sheer volume of data available today can be overwhelming. Decision-makers may find it difficult to sift through vast amounts of information to extract relevant insights. The effectiveness of this decision-making relies not just on collecting data but on the ability to analyze and interpret it effectively. This is where advanced analytics tools and data scientists become indispensable, helping to transform raw data into actionable insights.

Another significant challenge is the skills gap. Not all decision-makers have the expertise needed to work with data, especially when it comes to interpreting advanced analytics or building predictive models. While data literacy is becoming increasingly important across all industries, there is still a shortage of professionals with the necessary skills to navigate the complexities of big data. This gap can hinder the widespread adoption of data-driven decision-making and limit the effectiveness of organizations relying on it.

There are concerns related to privacy and security. As more data is collected especially personal or sensitive information organizations must ensure that they have strong systems in place to protect that data from breaches or misuse. Ethical concerns about the use of data, such as the potential for discrimination or bias in algorithms, also present challenges that need to be addressed in the development of data-driven systems.

Artificial intelligence, once a concept relegated to the realm of science fiction, has become a cornerstone of decision-making in a wide range of industries, including finance, healthcare, marketing, manufacturing, and logistics. At its core, it involves the creation of machines or systems that can learn, adapt, and perform tasks that traditionally required human intelligence, such as reasoning, problem-solving, and pattern recognition. The rapid advancement of AI technologies has opened new possibilities for automating decision-making and enhancing human cognition, allowing businesses and individuals to make smarter, more informed decisions.

The most important branch of AI in the context of decision-making is machine learning (ML), a subset of the technology that enables systems to learn from data without being explicitly programmed. Machine learning algorithms are designed to identify patterns, classify information, and predict future outcomes based on historical data. The more data these systems are exposed to, the better they can perform these tasks, effectively "learning" from experience. In practical terms, machine learning is used in a wide array of decision-making scenarios. For example, in financial services, these algorithms are used to predict stock market trends, detect fraudulent transactions, and automate credit scoring. The ability of machine learning algorithms to process large amounts of data and identify complex patterns that may not be immediately visible to human analysts has made it a powerful tool for decision-makers across various industries.

It also allows for continuous improvement. As the system processes more data over time, its predictions and decisions become more accurate. This is particularly valuable in environments where conditions are constantly changing, such as in e-commerce, where algorithms must adjust to shifting consumer behaviors, or in supply chain management, where demand patterns fluctuate unpredictably.

At the forefront of this innovation is deep learning, a more advanced subset of machine learning that involves neural networks with many layers (hence the term "deep"). These networks are modeled after the human brain, with interconnected nodes that can process information and learn from vast datasets. Deep learning has demonstrated remarkable success in tasks such as image recognition, speech processing, and natural language understanding, which were previously difficult for computers to master.

In decision-making, deep learning is particularly valuable in scenarios that involve unstructured data, such as text, images, or audio. For example, chatbots powered by deep learning can analyze customer inquiries and respond intelligently, helping businesses provide better customer service. Similarly, it is used in autonomous vehicles to process data from sensors and cameras, allowing the vehicle to make fast decisions on the road, such as avoiding obstacles or adjusting speed. Deep learning is also beginning to be used in areas like personalized marketing, where it can analyze consumer preferences and behavior across multiple platforms and recommend highly tailored products or services. By integrating deep learning with predictive analytics, organizations can make highly accurate predictions about consumer behavior and future trends, enabling them to make proactive decisions that anticipate market needs rather than reacting to them.

Predictive analytics refers to the use of historical data, statistical algorithms, and machine learning techniques to predict future events or outcomes. By analyzing patterns in data, predictive models can forecast trends, behavior, and risks, giving decision-makers the ability to act based on informed predictions. This forward-looking approach is a significant departure from traditional decision-making methods, which often relied on past experiences or intuition to anticipate future scenarios.

It leverages a variety of statistical methods and machine learning models, including regression analysis, decision trees, random forests, and support vector machines. Each of these models serves to uncover correlations and relationships in data that might not be immediately apparent. The process typically involves data collection, data cleaning, and model training, where the algorithm "learns" from historical data and uses that knowledge to make predictions. In business contexts, predictive analytics can be used for a variety of purposes such as customer churn prediction, demand forecasting and risk management.

Customer churn prediction involves analyzing customer behavior and purchase patterns, predictive models can identify which customers are most likely to leave, allowing businesses to take proactive measures to retain them. Demand forecasting refers to predictive analytics which helps organizations forecast demand for products or services, enabling them to optimize inventory levels and supply chain operations. Risk management involves predictive models which can identify potential risks and vulnerabilities, such as credit defaults or cybersecurity threats, and recommend actions to mitigate those risks before they escalate. Predictive analytics has become increasingly popular in industries where anticipating future events is crucial. For example, in finance, banks use predictive models to assess the likelihood of loan defaults, while in healthcare, predictive analytics helps hospitals forecast patient admissions, enabling them to manage resources and staffing effectively.

When combined with AI, predictive analytics becomes even more powerful. While predictive models are effective in forecasting future events, AI algorithms can enhance those predictions by automating decision-making and providing real-time insights. These models can also refine predictive models over time, adjusting to changing patterns in the data and improving their accuracy. In manufacturing, predictive analytics combined with AI can predict equipment failure before it occurs by analyzing historical performance data and identifying potential signs of wear or malfunction. This enables organizations to perform predictive maintenance, reducing downtime and improving operational efficiency.

The integration of AI and predictive analytics has opened up new possibilities for decision-making in various sectors. Below are several key examples of how these technologies are transforming decision-making processes across industries.

In healthcare, this technology and predictive analytics are used to improve patient care, resource allocation, and clinical decision-making. By analyzing large volumes of patient data, such as medical records, lab results, and imaging, predictive models can identify early warning signs of disease or predict potential health complications. For example, these systems are being used to predict the onset of conditions like sepsis, heart failure, and stroke, allowing doctors to intervene before the condition becomes critical. AI-powered diagnostic tools are also assisting healthcare professionals in making more accurate decisions. Radiologists, for instance, use the technology to analyze medical images, detecting abnormalities that may be missed by human eyes. These systems can suggest potential diagnoses, allowing doctors to make better-informed decisions and reduce diagnostic errors.

In the financial sector, AI and predictive analytics have revolutionized risk management, fraud detection, and investment strategies. Machine learning algorithms can analyze large volumes of transactional data in real time to identify patterns indicative of fraudulent activity, enabling banks to flag suspicious transactions and prevent financial crimes before they occur. These models also play a significant role in credit scoring, helping lenders assess the likelihood of a borrower defaulting on a loan. By analyzing a range of factors such as credit history, income levels, and behavioral data, these models can predict the creditworthiness of applicants more accurately than traditional methods, helping financial institutions make smarter lending decisions. In asset management, it is used to forecast stock prices, identify investment opportunities, and optimize portfolio allocations. Predictive analytics can also help mitigate risks in investment strategies by forecasting market trends and highlighting potential downturns.

In marketing, AI and predictive analytics have revolutionized how businesses understand consumer behavior and target their audiences. By analyzing vast amounts of consumer data such as website interactions, social media activity, and past purchasing behavior AI systems can predict what products or services a customer is likely to purchase next, allowing marketers to create highly personalized campaigns. Predictive analytics can also help businesses optimize pricing strategies, forecast sales trends, and determine the most effective channels for customer engagement. By making data-driven decisions, marketers can improve ROI on campaigns, reduce customer acquisition costs, and build stronger customer relationships.

While AI and predictive analytics offer significant advantages in decision-making, they are not without challenges. One of the primary concerns is the quality of data. AI models and predictive analytics algorithms are only as good as the data they are trained on. If the data is biased, incomplete, or inaccurate, the predictions and recommendations generated by these systems can be flawed. This underscores the importance of data governance, cleaning, and validation to ensure that decision-making is based on reliable information. Another challenge is the interpretability of these models, especially when it comes to deep learning systems. These models are often described as "black boxes" because their decision-making processes are not always transparent. This lack of interpretability can make it difficult for decision-makers to understand how AI arrived at a particular conclusion, which is especially problematic in sectors like healthcare or finance, where accountability and trust are paramount.

Finally, the ethical implications of AI-driven decision-making must be carefully considered. There are concerns about bias in AI algorithms, which can perpetuate existing inequalities in areas such as hiring, lending, and law enforcement. Ensuring that AI systems are fair, transparent, and accountable is critical to avoiding unintended consequences and maintaining public trust.

The integration of AI and predictive analytics into decision-making represents a monumental shift in how organizations and individuals approach problem-solving and strategy. These technologies enable faster, more accurate, and more effective decisions, allowing businesses to gain a competitive edge, improve efficiency, and reduce risks. However, their adoption requires careful attention to data quality, transparency, and ethics to ensure that these systems are used responsibly and effectively.

As the world becomes increasingly data-driven, decisions that were once based on intuition, experience, or qualitative judgment are now increasingly influenced by algorithms, machine learning models, and data analytics. These shifts are transforming industries, economies, and societies, offering new opportunities for efficiency, personalization, and insight.

In the digital economy, personal data is a valuable commodity. Companies collect and analyze data to personalize advertisements, predict consumer behavior, and optimize products and services. However, the boundary between useful personalization and intrusive surveillance is often blurry. In some cases, individuals may not have control over their data or even understand how it is being used. This can lead to feelings of powerlessness and mistrust in both companies and governments that collect and use this data. Further complicating this issue is the data-sharing between organizations. When personal data is shared between different entities, it increases the risk of unauthorized access, data breaches, or misuse of information. A lack of transparency about how data is handled and shared can erode public trust and raise ethical questions about consent and autonomy such as:

- Accountability and Responsibility: When algorithms make decisions, who is held responsible if something goes wrong? In traditional decision-making processes, accountability is usually tied to the human decision-makers who make the final call. But in a world where decisions are increasingly automated, this traditional framework of accountability becomes blurred. For example, if an autonomous vehicle makes a mistake that leads to an accident, or if a loan application is unfairly rejected by an algorithm, it may be unclear who is to blame, whether the developers of the algorithm, the company that uses it, or the system itself. One of the core ethical questions in this context is how to ensure accountability when decisions are made by machines. While algorithms can process and analyze vast amounts of data with remarkable speed, they lack human judgment and moral reasoning. This raises concerns about the moral responsibility of the individuals or organizations that create and deploy these systems. As decision-making becomes more reliant on data-driven tools, it is essential to establish clear frameworks of accountability that ensure that those who develop and deploy these tools are held responsible for the outcomes they generate.

- Transparency and Explain ability: The transparency of data-driven systems is another critical ethical issue. Many AI and machine learning models, especially those based on deep learning, function as "black boxes", meaning their decision-making processes are not easily understandable by humans. This lack of transparency can make it difficult for individuals to comprehend why certain decisions are made, particularly when those decisions affect their lives. Whether it's a credit score, a job application rejection, or a healthcare diagnosis, individuals have the right to know how decisions that impact them are made. The explain ability of AI models is a significant area of concern. If people are to trust data-driven systems, they need to understand how these systems work and why they arrive at certain conclusions. Without transparency, there is a risk of opacity, where decisions are made without individuals' understanding, creating mistrust and alienation. This challenge is particularly evident in areas like criminal justice, where predictive algorithms are used to assess the risk of recidivism. In both cases, the lack of explainable models can lead to skepticism, as individuals may feel that decisions are being made without human intervention or oversight.

To address these ethical concerns, it is crucial to establish clear and comprehensive ethical frameworks that guide the development and deployment of data-driven decision-making systems. These frameworks should ensure that decisions are made responsibly, transparently, and fairly, and that they respect individuals' privacy, autonomy, and dignity. Below are some key principles that should underpin such frameworks:

- Fairness and Non-Discrimination: A fundamental ethical principle in data-driven decision-making is fairness. This means ensuring that the data used to train algorithms is free from biases and that the resulting decisions do not disproportionately disadvantage any group based on characteristics like race, gender, age, or socio-economic status. It is essential that organizations take steps to identify and mitigate bias in both the data they collect and the algorithms they develop. This can involve auditing data for fairness, using bias-correction techniques, and continually monitoring the performance of AI models to ensure that they do not reinforce harmful stereotypes or discriminatory practices.

- Transparency: As mentioned earlier, transparency is critical in fostering trust in data-driven systems. Organizations should make efforts to ensure that AI models and decision-making algorithms are explainable to non-experts. This means developing methods for communicating how decisions are made in a way that is understandable and accessible to everyone impacted by those decisions. When individuals understand how an algorithm arrived at a particular decision, they are more likely to trust the system and feel confident that it is being used ethically.

- Privacy Protection and Data Security: The protection of individuals' privacy is another cornerstone of ethical data use. Organizations should adopt strict measures to safeguard personal data and ensure that it is only used for the purposes for which it was collected. This includes informed consent ensuring that individuals are aware of and agree to how their data will be used and ensuring that data is stored securely to protect against breaches or unauthorized access. Additionally, individuals should have the ability to control their data, including the right to delete or correct information that is inaccurate or no longer needed.

- Accountability and Governance: As decision-making becomes more automated, the question of accountability becomes even more important. Ethical frameworks should establish clear lines of responsibility for data-driven systems. This includes ensuring that organizations have mechanisms in place to monitor and audit AI models and data systems, particularly in areas where they may have significant social or economic impacts. Furthermore, those who develop or deploy AI models should be held responsible for the outcomes of these systems, especially if they result in harm to individuals or communities.

- Human Oversight: Although AI and data-driven models can make faster and more accurate decisions than humans, they should not replace human judgment altogether. It is essential to maintain human oversight in critical decision-making processes, particularly in sectors like healthcare, criminal justice, and finance. AI models should be viewed as tools to assist human decision-makers, rather than replace them entirely. Human expertise is still required to provide context, interpret data, and consider ethical implications in complex decision-making situations.

The rise of data-driven decision-making has opened up vast opportunities for innovation, efficiency, and insight. However, it has also introduced new ethical challenges that must be addressed to ensure that these systems are used responsibly and justly. Bias, privacy concerns, accountability, and transparency are just a few of the critical ethical issues that need to be carefully considered as data and AI systems become more deeply integrated into decision-making processes across industries.

To navigate these challenges, organizations, governments, and data scientists must commit to ethical principles that prioritize fairness, transparency, privacy, and accountability. By doing so, we can ensure that these decision-making benefits society as a whole, rather than exacerbating inequality or creating harm. As the power of AI and data continues to grow, it is our collective responsibility to shape a future where technology serves humanity, not the other way around.

CONCLUSION

As we reach the conclusion of this book, I want to pause and reflect on the journey we have just undertaken. We've explored the fascinating, intricate, and often transformative world of data from a variety of angles, through its language, its patterns, its ethical dilemmas, its predictive power, and its visual storytelling. We've peeled back the layers of raw numbers to uncover the hidden narratives they carry, the assumptions they reinforce, and the profound impact they can have on individuals, organizations, and entire societies.

This book has been about understanding data, not as a passive entity, but as a dynamic and powerful force that shapes how we view and interact with the world. Throughout the chapters, we've navigated the complexities of this force, dissecting it and analyzing it from multiple perspectives. Now, in this final section, I will attempt to bring all of these threads together into a coherent whole. We'll look back at the essential lessons we've learned, explore the open questions that remain, and challenge ourselves to think critically and creatively about how we move forward in this ever-evolving landscape.

Our journey began with an exploration of the very foundation of data: its language. Numbers are often seen as neutral, cold, and impersonal. But, as we have discovered, numbers are not inherently so. They are simply representations and symbols that carry meaning when placed within a context. The first key takeaway is that data is not self-explanatory. Numbers do not "speak for themselves" in the way that many may assume. Without thoughtful interpretation and analysis, they are little more than a jumble of digits. But with the right framework and the right questions, these numbers can start to tell compelling stories.

In the initial chapters of the book, we explored how understanding the language of data is essential for making sense of it. But it is not enough to simply know how to analyze data; we also need to know how to interpret it within a broader context. In other words, data is not just about numbers, it's about context, meaning, and relevance. Whether we are looking at sales figures, crime statistics, or health outcomes, we must always ask: What do these numbers truly mean, and what is the larger story they are trying to tell?

This leads us to the first major insight of this book: data is a language that must be learned and understood in depth. But, unlike natural languages, the language of data is highly structured, often driven by mathematical and statistical principles. To decode it, we must be conversant in the language of probability, correlation, and causality. We must learn to speak the language of analysis, visualization, and interpretation, where context and nuance are as important as the numbers themselves.

As we moved from the foundational elements of data to the art of interpretation, we saw how raw numbers could be transformed into rich narratives. This is where the true power of data lies not in its collection, but in its transformation into something meaningful. We learned that data alone cannot answer all our questions, but when combined with context, insights, and storytelling, it can reveal profound truths.

The transformation of raw numbers into narratives is a critical skill. In the world of data science, we are often called upon to take seemingly unrelated data points perhaps from different sources, over different time periods and weave them into a coherent story that helps others understand a situation or make better decisions. For example, a company might gather data on customer behaviors, purchase patterns, and demographic information. Alone, these pieces of data might not reveal much. But when these data points are combined and analyzed together, they can form a rich narrative about customer preferences, market trends, and potential opportunities.

At the heart of every insightful analysis lies a critical skill: asking the right questions. It is not enough to simply collect data; we must be deliberate in how we gather it and, more importantly, how we interpret it. In the chapters focused on this theme, we discussed how crucial it is to approach data with curiosity and skepticism, to ask questions that probe deeper and challenge assumptions. This process of inquiry drives the discovery of hidden patterns and relationships.

The skill of asking the right questions is an iterative process. It begins with curiosity, but it evolves as we gather more data and refine our understanding. As data scientists, we must recognize that our questions shape the results we obtain. For instance, a vague question like "What is the average income of people in this city?" may give us a quick answer, but it tells us little about the distribution of income or the social factors driving disparities. A better question might be, "How does income inequality in this city vary across different neighborhoods, and what are the underlying drivers?" This question opens the door to a more nuanced analysis and can uncover insights that are much more valuable in guiding policy decisions.

The real power of data comes from the ability to ask the right questions such as questions that uncover patterns, identify trends, and offer clarity in a world that often feels chaotic. In data science, the questions we ask are as important as the data we collect. In fact, often, the best data scientists are those who ask the most incisive and challenging questions, pushing the boundaries of conventional thinking.

We then moved into the realm of patterns and predictions, where we explored the idea that data allows us to see order where there seems to be none. In a chaotic world, data provides us with the tools to identify patterns whether in consumer behavior, disease outbreaks, or economic trends that allows us to make more informed predictions about the future. This chapter was about recognizing that data is not just a snapshot of the present but also a glimpse into the future. By analyzing historical data, we can forecast trends and outcomes with increasing accuracy.

But as we discussed, predictions are never certain. The future is inherently unpredictable, and even the most sophisticated models are subject to uncertainty. This is where the limits of prediction come into play. Data can help us make educated guesses, but it is essential to recognize that no model, no matter how advanced, is infallible. Understanding the limitations of our models and the uncertainty inherent in data is a key part of responsible data science.

A critical theme throughout this book has been the impact of bias on decision-making. From the way we collect data to how we interpret it, biases whether conscious or unconscious can skew our results and lead us to draw faulty conclusions. We have discussed how data is not neutral and it is shaped by the choices we make at every stage of its collection, analysis, and presentation. This is one of the most pressing ethical challenges in the field of data science today. As we continue to collect and analyze more data, we must be vigilant about the ways in which biases both explicit and implicit can creep into our models. How can we, as data scientists, safeguard against the pernicious effects of bias? And perhaps more importantly, how can we use data to promote fairness, inclusivity, and justice in our societies?

One of the most powerful tools in the data scientist's toolkit is visualization. As we saw in the chapters on data visualization, the ability to convey complex insights through clear, compelling visual representations is an essential skill for any data practitioner. Data visualizations whether in the form of charts, graphs, or infographics serve as a bridge between raw data and human understanding. They help to illuminate patterns, highlight trends, and make the unseen visible.

But visualization is not just about creating attractive graphics rather it's about telling a story with data. A well-crafted visualization can simplify complex data sets, turning them into something intuitive and accessible. It allows decision-makers to quickly grasp key insights and make informed choices. However, as we discussed, the power of visualization comes with a responsibility. Misleading visuals can distort the truth and misguide decision-making. Whether it's using misleading axes, inappropriate chart types, or omitting critical data, we must always be mindful of how we present our insights.

Perhaps the most significant thread running through this book has been the emphasis on ethics. As we saw, the power of data is undeniable, but it also comes with a heavy responsibility. Ethical decision-making is paramount in every stage of data work, from data collection to analysis, from visualization to interpretation.

Ethics is not a one-time consideration; it must be woven into the fabric of every data-driven decision we make. This involves not only ensuring the accuracy and integrity of the data but also safeguarding privacy, fairness, and accountability. Ethical concerns should be front and center in every conversation about data and its role in decision-making. As the use of data continues to grow, we must continue to ask critical questions about how it is used and whether its application is truly serving the common good.

Throughout the book, we've discussed how data science is not just for data scientists; it is a tool that can benefit everyone. In the final chapters, we shifted the focus to how we can all leverage data in our daily lives to make better decisions, whether at work, in our personal lives, or in our communities. Data, when understood and applied effectively, can empower individuals to make more informed, rational choices. In the age of information, data literacy is no longer a luxury but a necessity. Whether you're a business leader, a teacher, a healthcare professional, or a concerned citizen, the ability to understand and use data is becoming increasingly important. We must ensure that everyone has access to the tools, resources, and training they need to become more data-savvy, to interpret the data they encounter, and to make better decisions as a result.

We also explored the power of collaboration. In an increasingly complex world, no one person, team, or organization can possess all the answers. The most innovative, impactful solutions come from collaboration, where diverse perspectives, expertise, and experiences come together to create something greater than the sum of its parts.

Data science is a deeply collaborative field. Whether working in teams or engaging with stakeholders, the best data-driven decisions come from collective intelligence. But collaboration also brings challenges and communication, alignment, and trust must be built between different groups to ensure that data is used effectively. How can we build bridges between data scientists and the communities, organizations, and people who will benefit from the insights we generate?

Finally, we turned our gaze to the future. The future of decision-making is intertwined with the future of data. As technology advances, as data becomes more abundant, and as the tools to analyze it become more powerful, the role of data in shaping our decisions will continue to expand. But with this increased power comes greater responsibility.

How will we ensure that data is used ethically, transparently, and equitably? How will we safeguard against the risks of bias, misinformation, and misuse? How will we continue to adapt and innovate in this rapidly changing landscape?

The future, as always, is uncertain. But one thing is clear: data will continue to play an increasingly central role in how we understand the world and make decisions. It is up to all of us, data scientists, decision-makers, and citizens alike to ensure that we use this power wisely.

The journey of exploring data is never truly over. It is an evolving process, a never-ending cycle of learning, questioning, and discovering. As you close this book and look ahead, I challenge you to ask yourself: How will you use data in your life? How will you ensure that your decisions are informed by data, but also by ethical considerations, empathy, and a broader understanding of the world around you?

In the end, the story behind the numbers is not just about the numbers themselves. It is about how we, as individuals and as a society, choose to understand and use the data we collect. It is about the impact we can have when we take the time to ask the right questions, seek out the right answers, and approach data with curiosity, responsibility, and a deep sense of ethical obligation.

The future of decision-making depends on us. And that future is now.

www.ingramcontent.com/pod-product-compliance
Lightning Source LLC
LaVergne TN
LVHW092007090526
838202LV00001B/35